GENEROUS PRAISE

Extracted from my own Exercise 7.3

"You taught me to dive, to wish to be a mother, to find someone to grow as a couple with, to continue studying without stopping, to find myself, to trust in my strengths and to face my fears.
I saw your great determination in pursuing and making your dreams come true."

–Brenda.

"As time went by, your determination to keep going forward made you a woman who had nothing to do with the one that started the program, because on graduation day you gave a speech so great that I was truly amazed! Highlighting here that one of the strengths that I see in you is the determination to move forward and fulfill your goals."

–Erick

"When we started to do philosophy for children, you gave us the opportunity to approach the kids of a shanty town. It was an experience that marked Cindy and I. Since then, I have always thought that it is about giving an opportunity for thought to flourish among those who really need it. Then you had to leave, and you asked us to move on. I realized the great effort you were making to move forward with a cultural center in a high-marginal neighborhood. It has always been an honor to first study with you, and then be able to collaborate, even a little, with you on something so noble."

–Chacho

"You have a quiet strength and thirst for learning. Very evident in asking strangers to hang out with them for part of a day. A shared day of exploring between casual observers."

–Chris

"One day your car broke down, and nobody knew what it was. You were very young, it was your first car, and you just opened it. You disassembled the carburetor, put it back together and it worked! Just like that, I've seen you take the initiative and do things. They don't always work out the first time, but you always manage to make them work.

The one that has impacted me the most was when you took the whole family to the island in a boat. On our way back the wind was very strong, and we all knew we were in danger. But you kept joking, standing, giving instructions and controlling everything; to the point where it made us believe that it really wasn't that serious. Later, we confirmed that it had really been a dangerous situation. But not only did you know how to keep things in order, but you knew how to transmit the emotional state that you needed us to be in.

On a birthday party, there were problems among the children, and each parent was trying to defend their own. You controlled the kids, sat down with the grownups and led them to establish agreements and rules so that there would be better coexistence among the children."

—Tere

"I remember with love and vivid emotion your deep interest in the meaning of Greek mythology and Homeric literature. I remember with pleasure the discussions and logical links that you inferred from cosmogony and anthropocentric myths."

—Antonio

"While I worked with you, I watched your attitude of starting new projects with enthusiasm; projects that require an ability to learn and practice, and you carried them out with energy and concluded them in a stable way, although always facing obstacles along the way.

I see your great desire to help. What you did with Phonetic Intelligence went a little further; it was very remarkable. You identified a functional technology already developed and already tested and you had the vision to import it to Mexico - and even made it arrive to Peru - and implement it to effectively improve education in Mexico, in a way that did not raise opposition, and that did not generate discord; knowing how difficult it is to introduce any improvement in Mexican education."

—Eduardo

"I always remember when you impugned an unfair grading in college. Your work had all the specified requirements. It was an integral composition, well-structured and also poetic. The teacher did not agree with your position, despite it being well supported. It seemed easy, from the teacher's position of power, to disqualify your work. It seemed natural to you to follow an impugnation process, despite the leader's orthodox stance and the marked vertical hierarchy of that time. You followed all the steps marked by university procedures and the ruling was unanimous in your favor. I doubt that since your case (in 2007) something similar had happened. The research professors who evaluated your work recognized the quality of your essay. I recognized since then, and to date, the naturalness and temperance of your ethical procedures."

—Arely

"Thanks to your leadership, and the way you connected our team to key people, we were able to raise funds to build a so needed wall for an orphan children's shelter."

–Gaby

"That time when we were training higher grades teachers and, after evaluating their performance in the first part of it, you decided to innovate with a communication exercise, I doubted that they would respond, or have any gains from it. However, you knew how to lead them in a way that they even did ridiculous things without worrying! And in the end, everyone participated and had excellent gains. Your authority was unwavering!

In the presentation and training for the teachers of seven schools together, I witnessed the way you had them all attentive and participating. It was clear that they all understood. I really like the versatility with which you can be very serious and suddenly playful. And I like the way the audience responds to that.

More on a personal level, I see that you are always willing to listen to us, but what I admire most is the support you always give us; not only regarding ApTAC (our organization), but in matters that have nothing to do with work. You always have something to share with me, and I pay attention to you, and it works really well for me! I take you as a very good coach. I have grown a lot with you, personally and professionally. Now I proved that I can stand and expose calmly in front of 80+ people, and that I can see and solve situations. I thank you very much!

–Yadi

"In that very large group, where I was your student, you knew how to deal with each of our ways of being. You knew how to be patient and gave us activities that made us learn."

–Lizeth

"I still have a work you did for the philosophy of science symposium, which is a sign of your sharpness and perseverance that as a student you showed, a singular intellectual maturity; your seriousness and, at the same time, your concerns stood out from others. Your smile, and your kindness, all characteristics that I always admired of you and that have taken you so far, my dear Lucí, reaping successes. I hug you with my heart."

–Mónica

"I was surprised every time you started organizing a summer camp; and once it started, it was very cool to see the achievement that, very rapidly, each of those many kids were reaching. They always finished the snorkeling camp having so many advances.

I recognize how you did so much for us to have the best education inside and outside home. Although it was so hard for us, and sometimes we did not realize it, now looking back and seeing the results of that is something very, very satisfying! And that gives us lots of joy!"

–Rodrigo

"What impresses me the most about you is the ability you have to leave even the things you like most to achieve a greater good. For example, when you stopped diving to resume studies. That is what makes the difference.

I see that whoever has achieved great things in life, the great ones in history, have had that characteristic. Never has someone who has grown big, done it in a lukewarm way. You decide something and you go for it until the end. Now that I see you betting everything on your book, there will be no way it fails! Because I am sure that if that happens (if it fails), that will mean for you that it is not yet finished."

–Leonardo

The Superhero Lifestyle for Teachers

The step by step system to transcend
your time, money and relationship limitations to live a life
of freedom and fulfillment.

The events and conversations in this book have been set down to the best of the author's ability and from her own point of view; some names and details have been changed to protect the privacy of individuals.

This is for you to use and share. All that is asked in return is to name the source, so others can also benefit from this.

Designations used by companies to distinguish their products are often claimed as trademarks. All brand names and product names used in this book and on its cover are trade names, service marks, trademarks and registered trademarks of their respective owners. The publishers and the book are not associated with any product or vendor mentioned in this book. None of the companies referenced within the book have endorsed the book.

Lucía Briseño has no responsibility for the persistence or accuracy of URLs for external or third-party Internet Websites referred to in this publication and does not guarantee that any content on such Websites is, or will remain, accurate or appropriate.

First edition April 2020
Second edition January 2022

Illustrations by L. Odette González

ISBN 978-1-7338158-5-7 (hardcover)
ISBN 978-1-7338158-0-2 (paperback)
ISBN 978-1-7338158-1-9 (ebook)

For more information, address: lucia@ alianzasparatrascender.org

The Superhero Lifestyle for Teachers

The step by step system to transcend your time, money and relationship limitations to live a life of freedom and fulfillment.

LUCÍA BRISEÑO HARO

For my sons
RODRIGO and LEONARDO
The true masters in my life.

For my mom
TERE
Who always has a smile for me
…to say the least.

PREFACE

The greater the number of solutions for a problem, the further away you are from the real problem.

How many solutions exist now for the problem of education? How many people, organizations and governments are trying to solve it? And how many solutions have you managed to apply?

This is because what's being "solved" are the problems that arise from problems from previous problems.

When you clearly define the basic problem, then you find a basic and simple solution. But the problem has advanced so much and for so many generations that finding and applying the simple solution becomes the most complicated problem of all.

If education were to provide the right information and tools for the human being to live, develop and prosper individually and in harmony with others, very surely schools would not even exist as we know them now. Although, if we were to restructure everything to how it should be, we would have enormous chaos which would be practically impossible to organize. Surely, we would end up with an even bigger problem. Like my grantmom used to say "When a dress requires multiple patches, it is best to create it anew."

It's like a snowball - while trying to stop it, it would run over us and grow even bigger. This book does not intend to stop that snowball, but to create a new one that grows with those who share the idea of education as a natural way of life that benefits us all: as individuals, as well as groups.

The lifestyle that you will learn here is not only for teachers at school. In a way, every person is a teacher. This is a lifestyle for those who want to achieve a life of ethical freedom in which they can be the best version of themselves without being repressed by other people's expectations.

The information, the formulas and the tools that you will find are a concentration of half a century of life, enriched by 30 years of research focused on education.

I've learnt from very many authors through the years. With time, their ideas have become mine, or my original ideas have found support in them, to the point that I can't recall every name or reference to give credit to. Among them, Maria Montessori and L. Ron Hubbard have remained as my main pillars, since they were able to *really see us*, and develop processes and systems that truly work every single time.

Although influenced by others' ideas, everything in this book is my own interpretation of them; and it is what I have seen, analyzed, and concluded based on real experiences when applying their knowledge, methods and technologies – some of which may be named throughout the book.

This book is created for those teachers with deep vocation and conviction that there is a better way to educate; one focused on creating, developing, and innovating; turning back the idea of educating to form labor and politically educated entities.

We are on the threshold of an education without walls, in which you can choose guides and mentors according to your interests. This is what has led to the success of the famous dropouts. Their success does not lie in having left school, but in having continued their studies on their own.

The days of education as we know it today are numbered. It will take a few generations for the change to happen. It is time to prepare and learn to surf and ride this new wave, or slowly and painfully succumb along with the lives (students) entrusted to us.

Is this a prophecy? Take it as a founded prediction from someone who was born among teachers and whose life has been always permeated by educational aspects; from someone who has been a witness and participant in various educational processes and who keeps on researching about the origin, evolution, and future of education.

So, no. It is not prophecy as something esoteric. It is a prediction based on origins, development and trends.

I hope you're seeing this as good news; because it is!

It is the moment in which, as a teacher, you can develop the best of yourself and transmit it to those who share same interests. It is now that you can find your tribe and grow with them!

It will not be more about fitting-in forcibly because it is required by beliefs, good manners or by customs; but to find where, with whom, and how we can become free, grow, bear fruit and share.

I hope that you are as excited as I am to begin this journey!

I would love to be part of your tribe,
Lucía

ACKNOWLEDGMENTS

For it is the apprentice who gives birth to the masters, I first and foremost thank my sons Rodrigo and Leonardo, who are both to me: apprentices and masters.

My most profound gratitude and admiration to my Yoda, Víctor Hugo Arthur, who finally helped me to take the foot off the brake and pursue the "impossible".

Anik Singal and his team al Lurn, thank you for being the catalysts in this long-awaited dream.

To my dearest team at work, mainly to Yadira Valle –one of the most important people in my life– and Lorena López, my two right hands at work, dear friends, and the ones that don't let me lose hope.

Odette González for making this book pretty and fun with her illustrations.

Rosalba Gonzalez, not even the best writer would be able to put in words my love and gratitude for you. Even though our thoughts and beliefs can be radically different, you have supported me in ways that I didn't believe possible before. I recognize, and thank the amazing and loving being that you are!

Christine and Tom Clarke, my role models. Every time we've spent time together, magic has happened! My trip to India, and the making of this book, were much easier with your love and support.

The names and mentions in the stories along the book are my best way to thank those who have played an important role in this journey. Although, I own a special thanks to Alma Dávalos, who walked me into the Montessori world, in a way that I totally fell in love with it; being my foundation to pursue my crazy dream about education. You see, Alma? I did not forget my promise.

CONTENTS

Introduction 1
    Why Good Teachers Quit… or Wish They Could Quit 1
    What if Instead of Consuming Teachers with Trivial Problems, We Allowed Them to Foster Creativity? 1
    One Step at a Time 4
    The Root Problem 5
    Exercise 7
    When did I start being offended when someone called me a teacher?! 8
    Can't Live with Them, Can't Live without Them 9
    The Teacher in All of Us 9
    My Biggest Wakeup Call 11

PART I: THE FOUNDATION 15
Chapter 1: The Disappearing Woman 17
    The bucket of cold water that brought me back to the main problem 17
    How come education at school and home are two different things?! 19
    Formula #1: Stop, Think, And Act 21
    A historical paradigm change 23
    Exercise 1 25
Chapter 2: Your Superhero Style 26
    Somebody is watching you! 26
    Exercise 2.1 28
    Your very own superpowers 29
    There are basically three types of superheroes 32
    Exercise 2.2 33
Chapter 3: From Princess to Warrior to Scientist 36
    Everything is written in stone 37
    Teach by example 41
Chapter 4: Mission Impossible 43
    Blood, sweat and tears 43
    The safety net 44
    Save yourself first 44
    The good, the bad, and the confused: 47
    Not only the good ones have superpowers 49

Exercise 4.1 50
Exercise 4.2 51
3 Important notes 52
The best way to proceed 53

Chapter 5: The Edge 56
Let's do it the right way 58
How I got back on my feet 59
It is science 60
Formula #2: Make Things Happen 61
Exercise 5.1: Your magic wand 64
Exercise 5.2: Your magic wand II 65

Chapter 6: Authority 66
Insanity 66
Authority 67
Be the authority in your space… then expand your space 68
Find your Yoda, or better yet, your Yodas 69
You are the author of your goal! 71
Exercise 6: Your Yoda 72

PART II: THE STEPS 74

Chapter 7: Arithm-Ethic 76
How to apply it in our everyday life 78
Formula #3: Arithm-Ethics 79
Exercise 7.1: Your levels of progress 82
Exercise 7.2: Subtract to multiply 83
Exercise 7.3: Expansion is a natural tendency. 85
Exercise 7.4: Allies and enemies 86

Chapter 8: "Gadgets" and Kryptonite 88
Kryptonite 89
The strongest kryptonite: trying to help someone that doesn't want
to be helped. 89
A hidden type of kryptonite: to stop learning. 90
An understood type of kryptonite: lack of resources. 91
Exercise 8.1: Creating in abundance. 92
3 Main Gadgets 93
1. An armor and a weapon 93
2. A processing and control center 94
3. A cornucopia 96
A couple more things about the brain 97
Exercise 8.2: Clean and rewire your brain 98

How my gadgets worked for me 99
Chapter 9: Your 7 Areas of Action **101**
    The world vs your world 101
    More on Personal Integrity 108
Chapter 10: Reintegrating Your Integrity **110**
    Are we inherently good or evil? 111
    First me, or the others? 112
    When *first me* becomes evil 112
    The non-cooperative 114
    A couple of answers 115
    How to favor the cooperative 116
    Controlling the non-cooperative 116
Chapter 11: Time Management **119**
    Control is the key to efficiency 120
    Steps of an action cycle 121
    Controlling the self 124
    Exercise 11: Controlling personal action cycles 124
    Controlling others 125
Chapter 12: Money **128**
    The end of my second life in this lifetime 129
    Transcend Your Money Limitations 131
    5. Based on the previous points, ... 135
    Formula #5: Create Money Flows 136
    Step 1. Create income 136
    Step 2. Increase income 136
    Exercise 12.1 137
    Step 3. Save 139
    Step 4. Invest 139
    Exercise 12.2 140
    Step 5. Repeat 141
    Ascending spiral 142

PART III: THE GOAL **143**
Chapter 13: Now What? **145**
    Innovate or *die* 145
    Let it go 148
    Never-ending continuum 149
    Exercise 13.1: Main Red Flags Check List 150
    Stop 151
    Exercise 13.2: Completions 151

Chapter 14: Start – Continue – Stop – Repeat 152
    To keep in mind 153
    The Formulas 155
    More than words 157
Bonus 159
    24 Qualities That Geniuses Have In Common 159
About the Author 164

INTRODUCTION

Why Good Teachers Quit... or Wish They Could Quit

The hardest decision for a good teacher is to choose between their own well-being (their physical and mental health) and their students' futures. If you're here, you might already be facing that decision.

Teachers like you know that every day spent under the overwhelming conditions of teaching is a day closer to burnout. In the end, this will hurt both you and your students.

When you—when any teacher—thinks about quitting, you aren't looking to get away from the profession, but to get away from the burden of a dysfunctional system that does not allow you to truly exercise your profession. What you are really looking for is <u>freedom</u>.

Freedom is not about escaping or running away like a wild horse – even wild horses don't run wild all the time. They have habits and routines that help them survive. Let's understand freedom as the ability to create in the absence of barriers. As human beings we all have an inner desire, and a capacity to create. The more we create, the more alive we are. When our capacity to create is restricted, we begin to perish, and our mental and physical health can suffer.

What if Instead of Consuming Teachers with Trivial Problems, We Allowed Them to Foster Creativity?

My third-grade teacher had that scary look of a Salem witch: an elongated black figure in a pencil-shaped skirt that made her walk as if she had her knees tied together. She was the most feared teacher in the school!

...Feared by the students. Because when she was with the parents, and with the other teachers, she acted like a fix-it-all angel that "only does what's best for the children.

That was the year I learned not to speak, not to move, to do what was asked of me - even if I didn't understand it; Anyway, I learned how to be a "good girl". Also, that was the year I realized that school would no longer be fun... by the way, it was clear that my teacher was not very happy at school either.

Still, there were teachers that made my schooling experience bearable. Physical education teachers always brought me some joy!

Another example of a good subject teacher was my English teacher in high school, who also happened to be my scuba diving instructor. That's when English started to make sense to me. This teacher was as natural in the water as he was in the classroom. I'm unsure how, but he always managed to make his lessons as meaningful in the classroom as in real life.

That was an example of life that I wanted to follow. He looked happy all the time. Even in difficult times, he found solutions with a smile. In some way he reminded me of Guido, from the movie *"La vita è bella"*(1997), who shielded his son from the horrors of a concentration camp. We, the students, were his sons!

By the time I graduated, I had already lost interest in the rest of my classes, and only liked English and diving. The diving lessons at school were very basic and I was ready for more. So I finished high school and followed this teacher's example. I dedicated myself to diving for 20 years.

Regular education is based more on correcting errors and raising test scores than on fostering creative skills and abilities. This makes us feel like we will never be good enough. We grow up thinking that creativity is a gift exclusive to artists, when it is not! We were all born being creative beings. But, as we grow, that creativity is gradually inhibited so we can "fit in". Creativity can be recovered! It can be fostered and encouraged by healthy creative practices. What if you started devoting more creativity to building what you want, instead of having to fight against the things in your way? To do what you have always wanted to do, but that you have always waited for "better times" to start? To see your students turn into blissful and successful human beings?

Impossible? NO.

It is not impossible. That's what this book is about. **It is possible to create a life of freedom and fulfilment** if you have the right data and the right formulas. But, first of all, you must be ready to apply them.

The good news, or the bad news, is that we are creative by nature. It cannot be denied and it cannot be hidden.

Is that good news or bad news for you? Observe your life honestly and you will have the answer. It will be good news if you are enjoying your life, and you are aimed to fulfilling your goals and dreams.

If you are there, congratulations! You are are on the right path. Get ready to go even further! The data and formulas in this book will let you reinforce your own creativity to higher levels.

If you are not, then it's time to realize that it is you who have been creating what you don't want, only you've done this unconsciously; so far. Get ready to boost your potential in the right direction, and be amazed by the results! This book will guide you toward a life of success and fulfillment you might have thought impossible.

One Step at a Time

Let's look at a list of reasons why good teachers quit[1], and then find the hidden problems that cause each item in the list. The solution to any problem begins by discovering the root issues that cause them.

> 1. Challenging work conditions:
>
> *Too much work; too little time; tight budgets; miscommunications; impositions; lack of materials; inadequate facilities; bureaucracy and overwhelming expectations. As well as challenging students, parents, superiors, and colleagues...*
>
> 2. Not enough support, and not enough respect:
>
> *A belief that a teacher should give it all without asking for anything in return; a belief that a teacher does not have a life of their own; invalidations; unrealistic expectations; unfair evaluations; oppression; no space to grow...*
>
> 3. Testing and data collection:
>
> *Time consuming; inconsistent; removal of direct attention to students; feeling of doing someone else's job...*
>
> 4. No longer looking out for kids' best interests:
>
> *Too much work; too little time; bureaucracy; overwhelming expectations; challenging parents; non-supportive superiors and colleagues; unrealistic expectations; unfair evaluations; doing someone else's job...*
>
> 5. In the end, family takes priority:
>
> *The demands of attention from your own children, spouse, parents, or friends; the demands of attention from your own body (health, strength, energy); the demands of attention of your own self (personal and professional growth)...*

What do these items have in common? What thread links them together? If we can find that thread, we can begin the process of fixing the root that causes everything. If we can find that thread, we can aim to overcome the problem. So. What do they have in common?

1. There is way too much expected from teachers, almost to the point where

---

[1] Mulvahill, E. (2018, January). *Why Good Teachers Quit Teaching*. https://www.weareteachers.com/why-teachers-quit/

nobody considers them as human beings with personal needs and wants.
2. The notion that a teacher must listen to everybody, but almost nobody *really* listens to them.
3. A tight budget for schools means a tight budget for teachers, which separates schools from resources and teachers from freedom.

In short: antagonism among the educational community and its stakeholders, lack of authority, and lack of money are the common factors here.

How do we solve these three issues? How do we define them in a way that we can address them? For any problem to exist there must be two contrary forces – or ideas – of comparable magnitude, which are interlocked.

> The first: *burned-out teachers wanting to do good and have a balanced life.*
> The second: *false beliefs about education and educators, which make things worse every time they try to make them better.*

Let's remember that the teachers of today were students yesterday. They learned in the same, or even worse, conditions than their students now. But today, they are obligated to teach with expectations of the future. To teach things that never learned themselves! New educational models evolve and are released every year, each time with more information and communication technologies and leadership skills; while every day, I *still* see teachers who are not proficient in any new technology. A vast majority of them still educate as if all their students will leave school seeking jobs from past times.

Along their lives, teachers have been on both sides of the problem: as a student and as a teacher.

The Root Problem
The real issue is

a general lack of knowledge and capabilities to survive and progress as an individual, and as a member of society, in safety, freedom, and fulfilment.

But the education system does not do this. It does not grant the knowledge and capabilities that allow us to grow and thrive as people and souls. When students do not receive that knowledge, they will have trouble thriving and growing. They will continue to demand from the teachers (consciously or unconsciously) something that the teachers themselves may never have learned.

This applies to students of all ages, including teachers.

Since you did not receive that knowledge and did not develop those capabilities as a student, how can you survive and progress adequately now as an adult? Surviving does not mean barely making ends meet. That is slowly succumbing. As in the jungle, those who barely make it are prey! Survival can be defined as an impulse to persist over time. Survival is a long, long journey! And you can only embark on a long journey when you know that it's worth it... and are prepared to do it.

Would it be worth it if:
- ✓ you knew how to manage and control antagonistic forces?
- ✓ you were recognized as an authority in your field?
- ✓ money were not a problem for you?

If so, then let's move forward.

I'll will help you take the first step towards a life of safety, freedom, and fulfillment. The knowledge you need will be found as you read this book, do the exercises, and apply them to your everyday life. Your capabilities will grow as you continue applying what you've learned with discipline and commitment.

This is a long journey. **There is no magic pill; there is a magic process, and it takes time.**

So, before you turn to the next page, stand up. Stretch your body and shake, shake, **shake it**!

Now, take a deep breath and let's get started.

Exercise 0

What if you could attain a life full of safety, freedom, and fulfilment? What would it look like?

Make a drawing that's as detailed as possible of you, as a teacher, being safe, free, and fulfilled. Have fun. Do not limit yourself.

When did I start being offended when someone called me a teacher?!

To my surprise, on the very day I started writing this book, I found out that I was not the only one offended by that. While sharing my ideas with another writer, he displayed mixed feelings about loving to teach but not enjoy being called a teacher. And the more I observed others' reactions to the subject, the more I confirmed that this is a large phenomenon.

In Mexico (but not in every Spanish speaking country), *maestro* is widely used to refer to a teacher, at any level, from kindergarten to university. Someone who has obtained a master's degree is called 'maestro'. Additionally, there is "professor." In the US, a professor is a teacher of the highest rank in a college or university; and "profesor" (one *s*), in Mexico, is someone who dedicates themselves to education at any level, with no specialty required. The word means different things depending on where you are. But many people, using different words, have that same problem: they do not want to be called teachers!

That tells us that it is not the word that is the problem, but the meaning that we give to it.

Teacher: *"one who teaches," c. 1300; noun from teach, from Old English tǣċan ("to show, declare, demonstrate; teach, instruct, train; assign, prescribe, direct; warn; persuade").*

Maestro: *From Latin magister ("chief, teacher, leader"), from Old Latin magester, from mag- (as in magnus ("<u>great</u>")).*

In these two words, you can see there is a similar meaning—yet, we have two words. So we must think of the concepts. A concept is a mental representation that helps us to understand abstract ideas.

So, ultimately, *we* are the ones who give meaning to these words. What comes to our minds when we try to define "Teacher"?

- How should a teacher be? Who said so?
- Is this what we really want a teacher to be? What we, as humanity, need in someone to entrust the education of our race?
- How does each of us contribute to either preserve or increase the value of such an undervalued occupation?

Can't Live with Them, Can't Live without Them

I was born surrounded by teachers; many of my aunts were teachers. I loved spending hours with them, they always had fun activities and materials to share with me. Helping them prepare for school festivals was the best!

...Until I was not a child anymore.

Gradually, school lost its charm and became an obligation. The breaking point was in high school, when I asked my math teacher in what practical way I would apply arithmetic sequences to –something like that. It was a legitimate question, I was not trying to avoid the subject or to upset her... but she did get upset, and said:

<<To pass the exam! Is that practical enough for you?>>

Suddenly, I saw that answer in many of my teachers' minds every time I wanted to know how to take information from school and apply it in real life. I stopped asking questions, focused on passing exams, finished high school, **and stopped studying**.

As is true with many of you–if not every one of you–there was one teacher I fell in love with, more than a few I hated, a few I admired, a few I fought, a few who became friends, and many who I forgot. But, for sure, I learned something from each of them.

The biggest lesson now is to realize that teachers are real people trying to live normal and good lives, just like everybody else... *but they end up living a life of a superhero without the cape, without a Batcave, without gadgets and technology and, most importantly, without a Yoda to mentor them.*

The Teacher in each of Us

It is said that the best way to learn is by teaching. I also like to say that we teach what we need to learn. These statements may seem the same, but they're not. Let me explain:

To learn by teaching is a *conscious* process.
To teach what we need to learn is an *unconscious* process.

In the first case, we already have some knowledge, and we want to prove it or improve it; so, we teach somebody who knows less than we do.

In the second, we believe to have the ultimate truth, so we put it out there and argue with anybody who dares to disagree. We stick to our beliefs and look for every reason to prove others wrong. We are not, in this case, teaching what we need to learn. We are avoiding new learning by collecting only data that reinforces our "expert position"— even if we are the ones who are wrong. So if we dare to examine our own behaviors, we can see what we need to learn.

To learn by teaching. It is like, let's say, a lawyer who works in a law firm and dedicates 2 to 3 hours each week to teaching in a university. He is forced to stay up-to-date and keep himself one step ahead of his students. In order to teach, he must learn.

On the other hand, when we teach what we need to learn is like, let's say, a biologist researching *stable social associations among humpback whales*. He could be an introvert, *unconsciously*, trying to understand socialization. When he goes out and meet with people – if that happens – he will be able to quote every chapter and verse on how socialization works. He may not know it, but he is finding in whales what he cannot do with humans. If he were conscious of that, and used his findings to teach himself, his life would improve!

In a way, you can recognize those who've really mastered a subject by the way they share their knowledge. They do not go around criticizing and correcting everybody. They offer genuine help to those who ask for it.

While I can only guess about how this process works for others, I can tell you how it was for me. It happened backwards: it was first unconscious, and then became a conscious decision.

Since regular schoolteachers were not the role models I wanted, I started looking for prominent researchers and scientists, as well as for spiritual leaders who were not denying the physical universe.

At the age of 37 I went back to school, because I wanted to create an educational system that would help people to be happy and successful in every way. Since then, I have gained a lot of knowledge and obtained a lot of data. I learned that, most of the time, that knowledge and data was disconnected from the field it was trying to improve. For instance, while studying philosophy, I mainly faced many people with large egos, to the point where I ended up believing that *humanists were the ones that hated humans the most*.

As a Master's degree student, I had in my hands very valuable articles aimed to improve education - articles which may have never touched the ground due to a lack of resources or an excess of barriers.

Since I was 14, I have pursued spiritual growth through different cultures, beliefs and practices. I gained a lot in that process, but I was still unable to live successfully in my "real" day to day life. I was still struggling to:

- succeed at the different roles that I "had" to play – even in the spiritual groups
- stop living paycheck to paycheck
- pay my debts
- love and be loved – I was unsure of what this even was
- stay healthy and fit
- move towards my dreams.

Finally, when I turned 48, I started seeing the bigger picture— the masterpiece that was being built all this time. It was as if every experience, action, and bit of data collected along the way was a different piece of the same puzzle. But there were missing parts-- missing parts which I found in a certain technology and data that connected everything.

Finally, everything began to fall into place!

My Biggest Wakeup Call

In 1990, my first son was born. **I realized that I had become a teacher!**

...but I didn't like teachers!

I knew that there would not be a magic bubble protecting me and my children from the "cruel world". **I had to do something**, or they would go through the same system of enculturation (the gradual acquisition of the characteristics and norms of a culture or group by a person, a culture, etc.) instead of receiving a real education for **real life**. An education for real life is one which would include every important aspect of being human, not just those that makes someone an obedient student. It's good to be able to work with society, and work with the systems around you. But without lessons that focus on *you*, lessons that help *you* live *your* life, life lacks that self-satisfaction.

Therefore, as my child grew, I
- devoured every text I found on education

- visited every school in the city
- interviewed principals, teachers, and parents
- picked an awesome Montessori school
- committed myself to do what it took to give him, and eventually his brother, the best education they could get... *as I understood it back then*

As I learned, I started to share and teach others, both about education and about spirituality. They were natural consequences of each other. I did not really plan things to be that way.

Do you see? Unconsciously, **I was teaching what I needed to learn**. As I taught, I researched it so I could continue teaching.

Fast forward to today. What started as a need to be a good mother continued as lifelong research into education. It was not only about schools. It was *about the self as a unit; and all of humanity as a group; and much more.*

Along the way, I have found the mentors that I've needed, and I have, of course, made the most of every moment with them. Now I can clearly see a bright future while enjoying a blissful present.

Here is where **teaching to learn** enters the game. It has taken me almost 29 years of experience, research, investigation, pioneering non-traditional educative models, and hearing the hundreds of stories and testimonials of students and teachers with whom I have been in contact.

Now, this is what I have – and what I **want!** – to share with you so you can benefit and, hopefully, *go even further*.

I'm sure that many unexpected lessons will come to me as a consequence of writing this book. Right now, my biggest challenge is to help you realize **how important and valuable *you* are**, not only as a teacher, but as a human being. Count with me to become the best version of yourself you can be.

For that, I will be handing you key tools, technologies, and formulas to help you **find and develop your Superpowers**, so you will not have to worry again about your students. You will stop 'just teaching', and instead, you will naturally transmit valuable knowledge to them, and help each one of them become the best people they can become too.

PART I
THE FOUNDATION

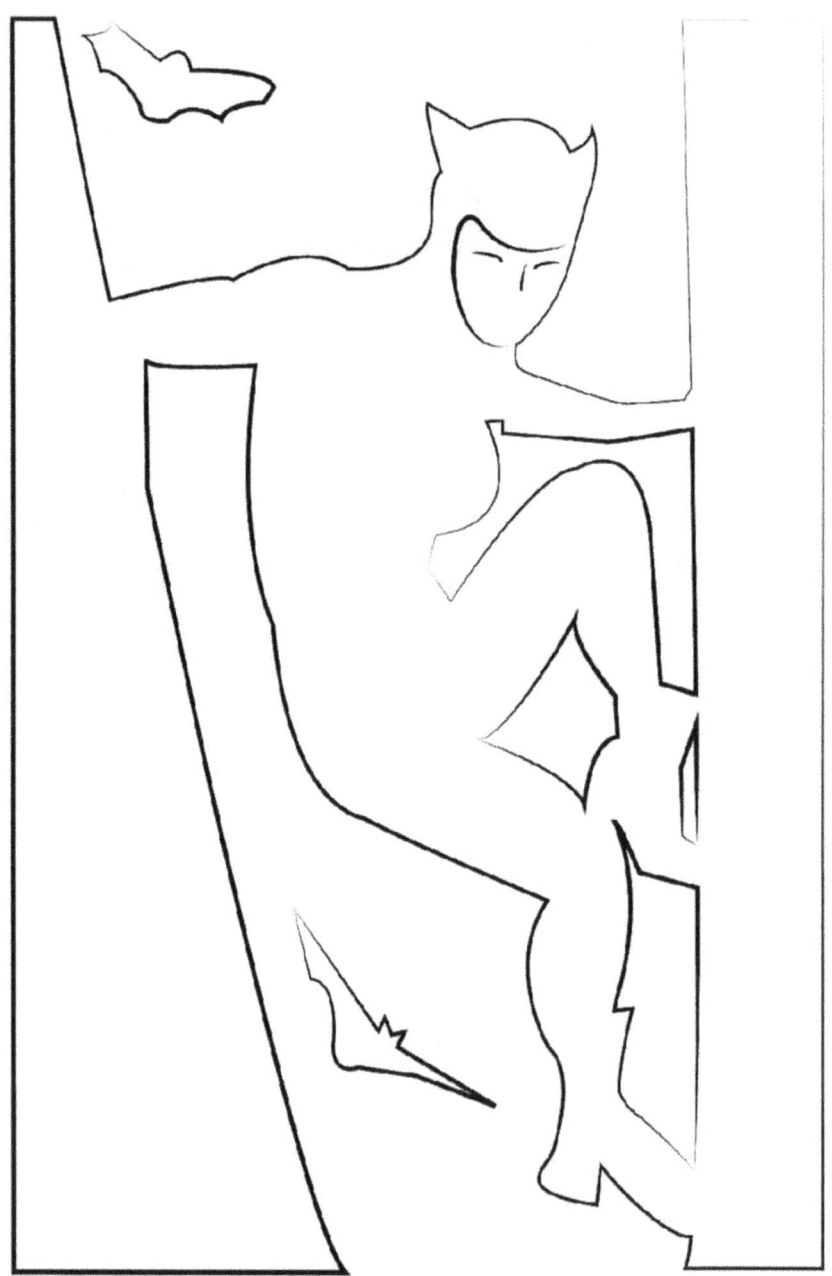

CHAPTER 1:
THE DISAPPEARING WOMAN

*"I knew the time would come when
you wouldn't be able to help me anymore."*

My son told me this when he was 13. First I had been everything for him, and now, I was on my way to disappearing from his life.

The bucket of cold water that brought me back to the main problem

I thought I had it all figured out: my kids were in good schools, practicing watersports with mom and dad, and having a good family life. What could go wrong?

The future could go wrong!

I saw myself back in time, when school lost its charm. I remembered all the things I gave up, not just because I did not have anyone to guide me to obtaining these dreams, but because many people persuaded me to fit in and forget about them. As my son grew up, I saw that same seed germinating in him!

First, it would be the time I could not help him with his 9th grade homework. Maybe later I would not be able to help him or his brother with finances, love, health… LIFE! All of it!

I needed to be ready to answer any questions they had — answers that would encourage him to remember his big dreams. If I couldn't, then I would disappear from my sons' lives, and wouldn't be able to help them.

There was no Google back then. Even if there had been, the problem was deeper than that. What was I teaching my son? …I mean, what was I *really* teaching him?

I could advise him to go to school, get good grades, and use those grades to be successful. I could tell him to be a well-behaved boy so he could become a happy adult.

However, I myself had dropped out of school. And while I could have given him this advice, I had spent years doing my best to convince myself that following the rules of society would – eventually — make me happy. But following the rules had not made me happy.

School did not help me to be successful. Even when I went back all the way to graduate school and took more courses, I was not any happier or any more successful than I had been at the start. Playing by society's rules, I realized that those rules were the wrong things to follow – they did not make me happy.

Enhancing my awareness, skills, freedom, and creativity did.

But for so long, I didn't know that. What I did know was to follow the instructions and beliefs of the "authorities" around me. Judging by their lives, it wasn't working for them either; none of them had the happy life they said would follow if they practiced what they preached.

…and there I was, repeating that same pattern and hoping it would work for my children. In the end, I had to be honest and tell them that I knew many things were wrong, and that I didn't have all the answers yet, but *for sure* I would not stop until I found them!

What I began to learn is that we should all trust in what is true for us. Not for others. We should measure if an action is right or wrong according to the results, *real results*. That is, what we have observed and experienced firsthand. That is: **if an action takes us closer to what we want, then it is correct; if it takes us further away from what we want, then it is wrong**. We are allowed to fail and make mistakes. The rules of the game are:

Do the best you can, with what you have, right where you are.

Once I learned the rules of the game I could see life from another angle, and see my own life in retrospect - it became clearer and simpler, and I don't know how I never saw it before! Learning how to observe results objectively helped me to see this. Learning how to observe the way results led to consequences — to see if they led to continuous and increasing improvement, or if they only led to momentary changes — was when I realized that observing is what I *had* to do.

But until I learned that, I had ups and downs all the time. Every time I was riding high, I felt convinced I was on the right path, and that success would just show up at my door. Those successes never lasted long. It felt like there was some strange force that did not let me go beyond a certain point. It was like when I had my diving school; it was a seasonal job. First season, I was successful and able to book students for nine months. Next season, I had to start all over again, instead of being able to expand or become more affluent than before. Because it worked once, I insisted on continuing forward and hoping my past success would repeat itself. It never did. Not the third time, nor the fourth and fifth, nor any of the other times. It was always nine months of success, and then starting again from scratch.

When success is not sustainable, when success does not lead to *greater* success, there is a problem; and every time you will be less willing to continue.

This wear and tear generally lead a person first to settle, then to get bored, and then to lose the motivation to try again; then stop creating. And <u>when a person stops creating, begins to disappear.</u>

My children, as well as my students, could listen to my teachings. But it was never what I told them that stuck. What stuck were the perceivable results of my own life, what my sons and students saw me doing and achieving... or, sometimes, when they noticed what I wasn't doing, and what I wasn't achieving.

It is not what I taught them. It is the parts of my life they saw that were, and still are, the most profound and permanent lessons I ever could have taught them.

How come education at school and home are two different things?!

The answer: each of them has different objectives. Worse yet: they have **two conflicting objectives!**

What you learn at school will always conflict with your personal life. School tells you that you must work hard and behave and be seriously formal five days a week, and then you can have two days off for your family and friends, and... What about pursuing dreams, following hobbies, or learning new skills? Where is the time for that?

The main problem is not the undervalued teaching profession. The problem is this:

The main purpose and intention of the educational system is one that teaches lessons about succeeding at **school**, not about **succeeding at life**. And **so many teachers** have been taught to think **about school-success and not life-success.**

Let's get clear on this important concept: *"the"* system, the one we all talk about, <u>is not</u> solely about governmental institutions; any system includes several elements within it. Including the educational system. Therefore you, your students, your parents, the school leaders, and the entire society—they are all part of the school system. **A system does not fail.** When a system does not give the expected results, what has failed is one of, or several of, the elements that compose it.

If we start from the premise that there is no single objective applicable to global education, then we do not even clearly know what we expect from that system. The same applies to particular demographics (such as a developing vs a developed country: the first focuses more on solving problems, the second on creating and innovating) and even – especially –, to families.

But before we dig in, we need to learn how to assess our immediate situation.

> A long while back, during a school trip for my son, we all went to visit a chicken farm. We decided to carpool to save resources and promote coexistence among families. My son and I, as well as another mother and child, were traveling with a boy we shall call Miguel, and his mother. Miguel was a badly behaved boy and considered the bully at school. On the way to the farm, he disturbed everyone in the car. We stopped at a red light at some point, and Miguel's mom grabbed her purse and started hitting Miguel with it while shouting:
> <<Why do you think I'm paying for a Montessori school? Don't they teach you to behave?>>
>
> At that very moment, I understood Miguel's misbehavior in school.

Later, I realized how much a situation like this can affect the whole system. And what a titanic endeavor it would be to fix it all!

But I also learned – and proved – that **not all was lost**. I learned that the first step to change something is to

STOP, THINK, and ACT.

Like I said, I proved it. Later, Miguel happened to attend one of my summer camps where the very first thing we taught everyone was to stop, think, and act. Miguel's transformation was remarkable! By the third day, he was completely integrated in a group of 43 children, and neither I, nor any of the instructors, ever had to worry about his behavior problems. The problems were gone.

As a side note, those concepts are very convenient in Spanish, because they are **P**ara, **P**iensa, y **P**rocede; so we had the 3P rule. For us speaking English, the mnemonic is STAnd.

Formula #1: Stop, Think, And Act (STAnd)

Take note, because this is your first formula—and it is the main formula we will return to throughout this book.

STOP

Things are not going to change if you continue repeating the same motions. Stop everything you've been doing that isn't working for *you*. Even if it has worked for other people, and/or worked for a long time... especially if it has worked for other people and a long time! If it is not working for you now, it is not going to work in the future!

Stop. Open yourself to change.

The first barrier to learning is the belief that we don't need new knowledge, or that we know everything. Unfortunately, this is especially true among teachers.

I don't blame you. Because, implicitly, you are required to hold onto fixed data, and to have answers to anything. You cannot *not* know everything. *But I am here to tell you: you don't have to know everything.*

Just stop, and pause, and give yourself permission to not know it all, and to be able to say <<I don't know>>. It's okay not to know everything. Nobody does.

In the same way, it's okay to say no. If you cannot help someone, or if helping them is going to hurt you greatly, be able to say "No." Be clear about the limits in your life that others must not break.

Now. Why take this moment to stop? Well, it's so you can

THINK

Now that you have stopped moving and broken the inertia of beliefs, customs, and practices that refused to let you think, you are ready to learn something new.

Investigate. Investigate everything you can about what you want to change. In this case, we will focus on education.

<u>Highly important</u>: Do not just investigate problems. Focus your attention completely on your goals, on what you see as being the purpose of it all! Do not think about what you wish to avoid. Focus on moving forward. If the gazelle thinks too much about the lion, the lion will catch it.

This is the core element of the formula. It is the basis of this entire book. In this chapter we will only address the first part of Think, which is to recognize the general environment. Then we will gradually approach each detail in depth.

ACT

Now that you have a good idea of the situation and you have spent time investigating everything and gathering information, it is time to act.

The better your preparation, the better your chances to succeed... but you must be ready to face failure. There is no way to foresee everything that can happen. Those who cannot consider failure cannot act, because they freeze, and spend time analyzing, thinking, and getting ready infinitely. **Sometimes you just must** *act.*

Begin to act, aware that at some point, you are going to fail. And when that happens, rejoice! Because you will find an out point that now you can put in. When you fail, you know what *not* to do. This is the way to make things happen! This is improvement!

Allow yourself to fail as many times as necessary. The only thing you must not do is fail in the same exact way. Define clearly what the failure was, and make a written statement of how to detect and/or prevent it from recurring.

Having said that, let's go back to the problem we are going to solve.

As we said, the main problem of the educational system is not the undervalued teaching profession. That is merely a consequence of a more essential problem, which we will say again here:

> The main purpose and intention of the educational system is to teach a student how to **succeed at school**, not at life.

We could examine this problem by going back to the industrial era and studying their educational systems. We could go back to any conquest in history and see what educational system the conquerors put into place. We could even go back to antiquity, when teaching was a selective thing for selective people. But you may already know that.

We have already established that we should look towards the future (your exercise 0). So let's focus on the paradigm shift we are facing right now.

A historical paradigm change

We have said, time and time again, that if the old way is not working for you, then you should find a new way.

A historical paradigm change

OLD PARADIGM	NEW PARADIGM
Have	Be
I	We
Boss	Leader
Hierarchy	Netarchy
Short Term	Long Term
Results based only	Process as important as results
Mostly routines	Mostly creativity
Focused on products	Focused on people

In short:

In the old paradigm, **the teacher** was meant to obey, stick to the rules and routines, give specific results, and save to retire. **The student** was meant to obey, stick to the rules and routines, give specific results, get a job, obey again, stick to yet more rules and routines, give more specific results, and save to retire.

In the new paradigm, **the teacher** is expected to analyze and discern; to hold onto a solid structure but create and innovate at the same time; to be good at teamwork while giving personalized attention to every student while being flexible with results; and able to always think about the long-term good. They are expected to have a happy and successful life. With that kind of education, with that kind of teacher, **the student** should be able to learn with ease, enjoy school, get along with others, be an entrepreneur, or have a job that could even be his hobby.

But... has someone ever asked how a teacher formed in the old paradigm can perform in the new one?

Answer: by developing their SUPERPOWERS!

Power: To act with great strength.

Super: More effective, more powerful, or more successful than usual.

The Disappearing Woman

Exercise 1

Now that you have a better idea of how to define a problem, write down that problem that you cannot stand anymore, and think about how you and others will benefit if the problem is solved.

[   ]

There! You have a good what and why to use your superpowers.

Don't worry about *how* that is going to be solved. You don't need to have the answer right now.

For now, focus on WHAT the problem is and WHY you would want to solve it. We'll work on HOW later.

This won't be an easy task. **But it surely will be worth it!**

CHAPTER 2:
YOUR SUPERHERO STYLE

I was lucky!

Years ago, I would spend time with a couple of friends when they vacationed where I lived. One time, they brought their little daughter with them, and that was the first time the girl and I had met.

By the third day, she had two braids and was wearing a hat… just as I did back then.

This instant change is an exception to the rule—changes are normally gradual—but it helped me see how it worked. The more time passes, and the more success you have, the more others will be willing to tell or show you how you have inspired them.

Somebody is watching you!
The same way you have copied others, others may be copying from you! And you may never know… although if you're lucky, you'll find out.

If you pay attention to the way you smile, the way you speak, how you move and dress, you will notice that you first copied it from someone else, and then gave it your own touch. That's how you created your own style; by adapting what you get from others. And that applies to thinking as well! But we'll get to that later.

It was most likely an unconscious process—so you may or may not like what you see, now that you know how it came about.
The good news is that now you can consciously design your own new style, and with a specific goal! By actively improving yourself, you'll become someone you **know** you want to be! If you don't like what you see now, you can change. If you do like what you see now, you can become even better!

Our students deserve, *and need,* teachers that show their inner power with the satisfaction and pride that comes from a well-used gift. They deserve it as much as you deserve, *and need,* to know that you are highly valuable and indispensable –

despite what others could have told you.

I've been lucky to have experienced that feeling more than once, when those who've learned from me have shared their experience, or I've seen myself have a good effect on them.

I'm so grateful for those who have come to me to tell me how, whether or not they were aware of it at first, something was transformed in their lives thanks to something that I said or did. There were even some that I had no idea were using me as inspiration!

> There was this young lady who came to me not long ago, out of the blue, just to tell me that the reason she became a diver was that she used to train Taekwondo next door to the dive shop I worked at when I was 17! I never saw her. I remember that dojo, and a bunch of kids training, but I never saw *her*. But she saw me: coming in and out of the shop, fixing the equipment, filling tanks with air, getting along with the divers... And she decided that she wanted that for herself.

What a responsibility!

When she came to me all those years later, I knew that I was not just teaching my students at school and my children. I was teaching anyone who was watching me! Every time there is someone near or around me, I am transmitting something; that is what I learned, and that is the most powerful way to teach.

This is not to scare you, but make you think about what it is that you are *really* teaching, or *transmitting*. Not just the things you know you are teaching, but the things you do in your day-to-day life. That is why it is so important, as a teacher, to make sure you present fulfillment in what you are teaching. Whether you know it or not, or want it or not; you are constantly influencing those around you. If you are happy with your life, you will naturally present that happiness. If you aren't happy, that will show no matter how good you think you are hiding it.

Now, let's thank the past for its teaching, and start having fun!

Exercise 2.1

This is your time. Get creative and **design your Superhero Style.**

Here is where you are going to choose your new style.

1. The left column is for your secret identity or social appearance, like Diana Prince (Wonder Woman), Clark Kent (Superman) or Bruce Wayne (Batman).
2. The right column is for the Superhero in you. The powerful, free and successful teacher with a special power that transforms lives.

Remmember to be creative beyond limitations. Aim to the stars and, at the least, you'll reach the sun. Aim to the sun, and you may end up in the moon.

Describe the new you that everyone will be able to see:	Describe your inner Superhero that will empower your social appearance:
Physically _____ _____ _____ Mentally _____ _____ _____ Emotionally _____ _____ _____	Physically _____ _____ _____ Mentally _____ _____ _____ Emotionally _____ _____ _____

Now, draw it!	Now, draw it!

Go one step further: make a collage of pictures or images of any aspect that you would like for your new style. And have fun doing it!

Your very own superpowers

One of the things I've enjoyed most in my life is scuba diving. For me, it was so easy and natural to "fly" under the water! To go effortlessly up, down, around; with or against the current; to be one more life among the sea life. I took it for granted that it would be the same for anyone.

Then I started working as a Divemaster.

> Once, a couple of tourists booked an introductory diving session. Usually, these lessons start with a very basic on-land instruction, then getting familiar with the experience in a pool where you can stand with your face out of the water. Then you get into the sea. But this was a shorter session—straight onto the ocean from a boat! And there we were, the two of them almost panicking, glued to the anchor rope, and there I was, trying to get their attention and make them follow my instructions.
>
> He, as a "good husband", was telling her what to do (while he himself was out of

control). She, as a "good wife", was pretending to listen to him to not make him mad, but wishing he would shut up.

There we were. Three people speaking ... but not communicating.

At the time I was 19 years old, and had been taught to respect others and not to interrupt; especially if they were older. So my ability to verbally communicate was quite deficient – and they weren't great communicators, either. But under the surface, I had total control. That was my environment. That was where I was totally me.

I took control. By acting and doing, and communicating with my eyes, hands and posture, I was able to really show them in a way I was not able to with speech alone. Without a word, and with *very* firm intention and control, I put the regulators into their mouths – first in his, of course – and took them down to a fantastic dive tour. The next day, they stopped by the dive shop and left this in the testimonial book:

"In our first diving experience, Lucy took us from high anxiety to high fun! She knows how to teach. We are both teachers and can tell when we see one."

I would have never thought that of myself at 19! They made it possible for me to see how I was viewed.

There was my Superpower! ... right?

I thought my Superpower was teaching, just like they said... but it was not. Later, I found out that my superpower was being able to notice things.

What happened that day was that we all connected beyond words, beliefs, and judgements. There was a point where the three of us wanted the same thing. I was able to see that. So we went back to basics, got rid of any unnecessary action... and voilà!

It took me years to realize that I was seeing things that others didn't. They seemed so obvious for me that it was so frustrating that the others "pretended" not to see them. It is like reading between lines – to see what connects us all, rather than what makes us different and separates us. It is not only good to be different, but also necessary; nevertheless our similarities are what allow us to communicate and connect; our similarities are what make us feel, enjoy, and create together. Our similarities are what help us live.

Why did it take so long?
Because it was not always like <<let me see you with my magic eyes and control the situation>>. That worked for me only under the water; that was my domain. There, I had the authority because I knew exactly what I was doing, so, I was transmitting. I was doing what I enjoyed most, and I was doing it well. My main interest was that each person in my charge could see what I was seeing, and feel what I was feeling. It was natural for me.

On the ground, the story changed. There were too many elements out of my knowledge, limits and, therefore, out of my control. Though I could *see* the essence of everything above ground—I could see where everything connected, and where all things could be done effortlessly—it was not my domain. The social and cultural rules I'd learned didn't include speaking up, so for so long, I caved in and did my best to fit in. Even if I could *see* where people were similar in needs, wants and dreams; I did not have the authority to act on it — to even recognize that I was seeing the right thing.

To make something real, all that is needed is agreement between people that something is real. Therefore, the more people that agree with something, the more 'real' that something is. Being real does not mean that something is true. For lots of people it is *real* that there is no education out of a regular school (social agreement). While for many others it is *true* that there are other ways (personal experience).

When you are able to see the truth, you realize all the "realities" of a situation...and it can become overwhelming and frustrating to try to reveal the truths you *do* see.

In the story I just told you, I discovered the superpower that I had to develop (teaching) in order to make the most use of the superpower with which I was born (awareness). The things I was able to see were true for me; but because I hadn't shown them to anyone else, I had no agreement with others; so they were not real. Yet.

Once I trusted my own truths, reinforced my superpowers, and acted in accordance with my truths, over time, my truths, my superpowers, and my authority began to be real for me and for others. When I was able to transmit to other people, without having to say what my power was, was when **what I see became real!**

Not all superpowers are like that. They are different for every person; and every person, surely, has more than one. There also can be combinations, a dominant power, or some eventual power that will help us overcome a specific situation. The most important thing is that they are true for you! And that you can strengthen them until they become reality.

Once everyone knows your truth — and acknowledges it — then what was a personal truth can become something that is real for others.

What a way to create a life! Right?

There are basically three types of superheroes

1. Born with superpowers: like Superman or Thor.
2. Developed superpowers due to a traumatic event: like Batman or Spiderman.
3. Designed superpowers: Black Panther, or Jake Sully from *Avatar*.

In any case, any superhero goes through **four stages**:

1. Finding/recognizing the superpower
2. Getting control over it
3. Hiding it from the normal people
4. Using it to serve others

By now, you may have a teaching superpower trying to show itself. Let's boost it by going deeper into this list, and seeing where your superpower came from.

Type 1. Born with it
Since you were in kindergarten, you could sense that there were things that just didn't feel right. You had fun and happy dreams, and wanted to explore, and try new things, and you knew you had the power to do it... but it didn't seem to fit well in the adults' world. Including in your teachers' worlds.

You grew up holding that inner power in check, and kept it dormant. And it's still there, waiting to be awakened.

Type 2. Developed it
There was an event that marked your life in such a significant way that things were not the same after that. You changed! And everything around you seemed to change too. You made decisions and developed abilities and capabilities that you didn't previously have, or that weren't strong enough before.

It may have happened when you were a student, or in your personal life, or in your life as a teacher trying to do your best and struggling due to bureaucratic regulations, unaligned authority, or problematic colleagues. So, you had to create a different approach (a different power) to address your problems.

Type 3. Created by design
You met someone, either real or fictitious, who inspired you so profoundly that you decided to become like him or her. The way that person addressed education was so unique and effective that you chose to replicate it. It can also be a combination of models, methods, and techniques.

You may find you have superpowers that fit more than one of these lists… or all three of them!

In that case, I recommend you weigh your powers and see if there is one that, at the end, is made stronger by the others. Like me thinking that my power was teaching, when it was not! It was awareness, which allowed me to transmit and motivate others to do something by transmitting techniques and authority. I, looking for ways to improve education, was really building my tools and gadgets towards Stage 4—learning to use my powers to serve others.

If you are still not sure about your main superpower, going through the following stages will help.

The stages
Stage 1. Finding/recognizing your superpower
Exercise 2.2
Go through the list and write your answers:

- What is the one thing that you enjoy the most when teaching?

  _____

- What methods have you have tried which have achieved effective results, but you haven't shared, or don't do openly, because you are afraid that others would not agree with you, or would criticize your methods?

  _____

- What is it that you see that can be improved – that you know how to improve – which nobody else can see or avoid seeing?

  _____

- What is that something that you stopped pursuing because somebody told you to be realistic and to put your feet on the ground?

_____

- What have other people, especially your students, recognized in you?

_____

- If you were to give yourself a teaching superpower, what would it be? (Don't "put your feet on the ground"—*this is your chance to dream big*).

_____

Now, go back to your answers and see what they have in common. That common link... is your Superpower!

Stage 2. Learning how to control it

Even Superman had to recognize his superpowers and learn how to use them responsibly.

Imagine what could happen if the Human Torch, or The Hulk, were not able to control their powers!

In the same way, we can hurt others if we are not careful. And worst of all, we can hurt ourselves! Because at first we think we are doing good, but others do not react well, so we start cutting communication to the point that we cave-in, become introverts, and then convince ourselves that it is a good thing to be alone. We become weak when *others* react negatively to our powers, instead of building our strength from the inside.

To control your superpower does not mean to stop it. It means to:

1. Fully recognize it
2. Decide where, when, and how to use it
3. Use it to achieve specific goals

Stage 3. Hide it from the normal people

Normal: ordinary or usual; what is expected.

Ordinary people don't like extra-ordinary actions happening near them. But everyone, even those who don't like surprises, is amazed by a superhero!

Therefore, at the beginning, it is better not to make your superpower too obvious. Superpowers are not things to brag about, but things to help you first, then serve others.

Besides that - and this is especially true in traditional educational systems - superheroes are not always welcome (sadly).

Remember Spiderman or Batman. With time, some of their loved ones got to know who they were. But, by that time, the service they had performed backed them up, and gave them authority as Superheroes. They did not tell their loved ones their powers until *after* they had gained authority by transmitting Goodness.

Just imagine if Peter Parker had met Mary Jane before spending a lot of time as Spiderman, and had told her that he would put on a bright jumpsuit and a mask to go after the bad guys... What had you done if you were Mary Jane? You would have run away!

In the same way, the people closest to you think that they are protecting you every time they ask you to stay in the "safe" zone... even though the "safe" zone is the MOST dangerous place to be! But we'll get there in due time.

Stage 4. Use it to serve others
This is the most effective way to serve yourself.

Here is an example of how it works:

> "Jeevetha, a 13-year-old HoPE Hero from Puducherrymedu village (India), wrote a petition to her District Collector requesting a bus facility for her village. Impressed by her leadership, the Collector passed orders for buses to be run during school hours. Now, Jeevetha and children of her village need not walk 6 kilometers every day to their school."[2]

This girl found a problem that was affecting all the students in her village – including her. She took the initiative (a great superpower) and then *took action* (which is how we manifest our powers!). She solved the problem for others and helped herself, not only by not having to walk to school, but by reinforcing her superpowers. She made her power real for herself and for others around her... and next time, will be able to use it again with more ease.

So, how do you apply it? That is what we have to talk about next. How do we apply our superpowers to help others, and ourselves, without burning ourselves out? Let's find out.

---

[2] https://www.tripurafoundation.org/press-release/

CHAPTER 3:
FROM PRINCESS TO WARRIOR TO SCIENTIST

Wonder Woman was raised first as a princess. She learned about social protocol, good behavior, and love and peace. But after being gifted the gods' powers, which included strength, wisdom, courage, and a love for the truth--sooner or later she had to escape the limitations of society, and go out into the rest of the world. She had no idea how awful the real world could be. The contrast between what she knew, what she thought, and what she faced was more frustrating, disturbing, and painful than she expected. This is how, in the end, rational observations led her to find a balance and a path to follow. Hence, Wonder Woman could *live* in the world as Wonder Woman, and do good while she did, rather than just fulfill individual goals.

Shoulds Vs Wants… And a MUST

I had always wanted to be a backpacker… *but not at the age of 45, in debt, with no job and no home to come back to.*

Why at 45, and not at 19, when I first wanted to? Well, at, 19 I was looking for adventure. But moral codes and cultural beliefs stopped me from traveling while I was young. But, later, ethics was finally setting me free.

Now I was looking for answers that would, finally, lead me to success. What could go wrong? When I left home, I had contacts. I had a goal. A job in progress in the research department of the Senate, working for an international foundation, and would live with a close friend in Mexico City. I had a plan! This journey would lead me to those answers, then to success—to freedom, to be myself, and to do everything I had always wanted to do!

However, even though I worked on every detail of my plan for months, it didn't go as expected.

I didn't end up in Mexico City. I ended up in Guadalajara, the second largest city in Mexico, with nothing but a backpack and a suitcase. I lost my job a few days after starting my journey, and my "friend" changed her plans, so I had no place to live.

How did I end up there?

I'm glad you asked!

Everything is written in stone
...is it? Even if it is, who cares?!

Guilty as charged... I did. I resigned myself to believe that my whole life had been decided by something or someone else; some kind of superior power that I dared not contradict.

I grew up a well-behaved girl who would not dare to disobey. I continued playing by the rules as I became an adult. My main goal was to make sure I was playing each of my roles to the letter, because I was told that that was the right way. If I dared to do otherwise, very bad things would happen to me and to the ones I loved.

Nobody promised that I would be happy ...but at least I would be a good woman in society and go to heaven when I died. If that was the way it was written in the moral codes and the rules of the society, who was I to say otherwise? And if that was not enough, there were my spiritual pursuits: the idea that everything was written in higher, divine spheres, and that free will only applied within the limits of what was written in those spheres. I was trapped between human and divine precepts.

On the other hand, there was a free-willed me who loved nature, loved people, and loved to see that things could be different! People could be free from hard rules, and could create for their good and the good of others. There were times when, in my mind, I could be inventing and reinventing my life at will. It was just beautiful, and it seemed so real! Most of the time, these moments would pass, and I convinced myself to come back from Lucyland and behave as a grown up.

...But sometimes, I stayed in the fairy tale. When I truly believed something was good, even if it broke the rules, and I went for it no matter what; those were the times I've had my greatest successes!

How many times, as a teacher, have you felt that you should be letting your students dream, and make mistakes, and create their own rules? How often are your actions guided mostly by set precepts, and not by real-time needs and wants?

We are supposed to teach our students how they should act, right? They should obey and play by the rules. They should not be free, and should not create their own way—they should only create the way they are told. But where did that belief come from? It does not seem to work for anyone. It's insane!

We repeat patterns simply because that's the way it has always been done for many years, or because we were taught that this is how it **should** be. And, oh boy, it's hard to even think about changing those rules! It requires responsibility and self-determinism! And nobody taught us that when we were little.

But, if by some lucky spark of self-awareness we decide to create a new path, the very first thing that happens is that most of the people around us will tell us that we are wrong. Some will relate, but will say nothing that could contradict the status quo. But if you continue moving forward, you will find support. You will find others who not only think like you, but who seek transformation too.

What should we be doing? What should we be teaching? And... what the heck is "should"?
Should is a word used to suggest that something is inevitable — even if it is not. So, our brain is programed to obey, or feel compelled to do what accompanies "should". Quite often we don't even question it! But if you think about it, behind every "should" there is somebody with certain beliefs and goals that (maybe) are not necessary for the greatest good.

The funny thing is that we overload ourselves with "shoulds", and believe that following those "shoulds" will make us *look* responsible, important, or mature. I know! I was an expert doing that; and I still see, literally, hundreds of teachers doing it and feeling proud of it!

A second-grade teacher in a training that I conducted last year, suddenly exclaimed "I just realized that I "have" to be a know-it-all! I feel that I should be able to answer any question, be it at school, at home, or even with friends. Otherwise, I would be failing as a teacher." What an unnecessary burden!

It is one of the heaviest burdens that we have blindly accepted since childhood. We are constantly told that we must know everything, do everything correctly, and never make mistakes. But who said that in the first place? It doesn't even make sense. It's not natural. The only way we can learn is by experiencing mistakes and **learning from them**. After all, true learning is not found by achieving specific objectives, but in experiencing the process that led to the result.

Next time you have a "should", instead of reacting to it, **STAnd! Stop, Think, and Act**.
  S= do not follow it blindly. Stop and carefully observe the situation.
  T= Think whose "should" it is and what is its purpose. Will that purpose *really* be obtained by doing this? Do you agree with it? What if you don't do it, or do it differently?
  A= continue with the action, or stop it, or adjust it, according to your answers in **T**.

The best way to evaluate the purpose of an action is to know if it is driven by moral or ethical considerations.

Ethics and morals tend to be used synonymously, but they are not synonyms. They are used that way because both are standards of good or bad behavior, and are based on personal beliefs rather than on law. But they differ in their scope.

A moral is an agreed upon code of norms that is considered good for directing or judging the behavior of people in a community. Morals are often meant to guarantee the survival of a specific group in a specific period under specific circumstances. These codes can, in the end, become laws.

But, if that period ends or the circumstances change, and the codes remain the same, then instead of guaranteeing survival, those codes, norms, and laws begin to destroy the same group that they were meant to protect!

For instance, in the Middle Ages, the moral code dictated cutting the hands of thieves and the tongues out of liars. Imagine if it had remained until these days!

At school, a moral code that says "wear this uniform!" may work fine in a metropolitan area, but not in a rural town. Also, a moral code will tell you to be nice to everyone, while ethics will tell you not to be nice when someone is causing you harm. Ethics will prompt you to protect yourself and, if necessary, to fight back.

Ethics are rationalized morals.

Ethics is personal; morality is for groups.

Usually, when we are repeating a pattern that does not work, does not make us feel good, and that costs a lot to change, we are facing a moral that has outlived its use. It needs to be reevaluated and turn into an ethical action.

Shoulds are usually imposed by moral codes, while ethical actions move us to **our wants**. Consider this…

When we **should** go to work, we may not want to. We feel like we have to. When we **should** go back home, we do it because we feel like there is responsibility and obligation. If we **should** spend time with friends, it may not be because we really enjoy it. It may be because we feel that, in order to be a friend, we must do this thing… but what about when we *want* these things?

When we *want* to go to work, it is because we enjoy it, and is helping us to be better; and there we may have a good group to grow with. When we *want* to go back home it is because home is where we are filled with love; because it is our safe place. If we *want* to dance, or rest, or hang with friends, it is because it makes us feel alive! It fills us with love!

It is as easy as that!

Once you recognize the differences and start making your decisions based on what is ethical, and not only what is moral, your life will improve dramatically!

The moral codes will continue to exist, and they are not necessarily bad. In fact, they can be quite convenient. They *will be* convenient, and *will* work in your favor and in your network's favor, to the extent that you can recognize them, keep them within their limits, and update them when necessary. Moral codes are great!…when they stay in place and updated.

This realization is what moved me forward when I turned 45. It is what made me leave home, and attempt to start a new life, in a new place. I knew it would come with a high price, but not as high as inaction would have been.

This time I was going to build my life based on what was ethical; it would be based on my wants, and not on some idea of "should"; it would be based on what was true to me. I was going to rewrite my own story and make my own mistakes without having to justify them to anyone, and without feeling guilty for not following traditional rules. I was determined to achieve the "unachievable"! To speak my truth with the best language I knew: by action.

So, my "must" arose.

Wait! You may say: Aren't "should do" and "must do" the same?
In a way, they are. What makes them different is whether or not something is imposed, or self-determined. If something is imposed on you, it is a "should". But if you firmly determine a goal, then achieving it becomes a *must*. Now that I had gotten rid of the imposed "shoulds, I was ready to choose my own must.

While I was helping others find and go after their dreams, I had never consciously pursued my own dreams. I kept on thinking that it would always be a matter of time: something I would do as soon as I finished this, or sent that, once this or that happened... So I kept on postponing them again and again.

Teach by example
The best teachers I have had are those who had already accomplished what I wanted to accomplish myself. They learned it by studying, experiencing, making mistakes, and finally, succeeding.

But, unfortunately, we get to these teachers late in life. If we are lucky, we may find some during university.

You may think that to teach elementary school you don't need to know much. It's just the basics. But that's only if you consider elementary education as only learning to read and write. If you think that education is more than academic knowledge, then things change.

From kindergarten to high school, we mostly have teachers telling us to do things that *they don't do themselves*. They tell us to study "to be someone in life" (never defining what that even means) and be successful. But, man! It is hard to believe them when you see that most of them are unsatisfied with their own lives and their own jobs. They tell us to behave and get along with our classmates while they gossip and talk behind peoples' backs!

I learned first-hand that this elementary education didn't have to be "just the basics".

While teaching in high school and university, the common factor among students was that they were full of energy, potential, and dreams; but totally lost in confusion.

> There was this boy in a high school class I taught, let's call him David, who thought he should become a lawyer because he was told that it was the best choice he had. But he had entrepreneurial dreams. Since I had knowledge about administration and entrepreneurship, I gave him some advice. A few months later, bam! He was studying administration in the University where I happened to be his teacher again. He was learning skills that would help him pursue his dreams.

I felt totally responsible for that!

Although I was happy because he seemed more alive than when he'd said he was going to be a lawyer, I felt unable to take him any further, because while I had some experience, theories and plans, I was not acting towards my own dreams.

At home, something similar was happening: I thought I was giving my children the best education. I was being very careful to open their panorama of options and great things that they could do. And they were consciously doing their very best. But unconsciously, they were repeating similar patterns and mistakes over and over again... patterns and mistakes I had made.

I had that "analysis-paralysis" block. I was already a skilled entrepreneur in Excel, and a celebrity in PowerPoint; but in real life, there was a lot I still had to learn.

If I wanted my sons to change for their better, I had to change myself first. If I wanted my children and my students to go and achieve their dreams, I had to do it myself first.

Pursuing my dreams moved to the top of the list. It became **my must**.
In three months I sold, gave away, and even burned almost all my belongings; said goodbye to the man who had been my husband until that day; had the hardest conversations I've had with my sons; put what would be most indispensable for me in a suitcase and a backpack, and then left the city.

This time I was going to teach by example.

This was the point of no return.

CHAPTER 4:
MISSION IMPOSSIBLE

There I was in Guadalajara, with a suitcase and a backpack, no place to stay, no job, and in debt.

This is not what I had planned. I told you! I was supposed to be in Mexico City staying with a good friend, working for an international organization, and on my way to get a very good job in the research arm of the senate of Mexico.

Full of energy and hope, I had left the city where I had built my life over 30 years. I was sure that all I had learned before about succeeding in life would finally materialize. That if it hadn't happened before, it was because I hadn't made that famous leap of faith.

I jumped into the abyss and the parachute did not open.

My "friend" changed her mind; the organization was afraid that I would not perform well in Mexico City, so they withdrew their support; and I didn't get the job in the senate – which was really frustrating, because I knew I was totally qualified for that, but was rejected without any explanation.

Blood, sweat and tears

For now, it is enough to tell you that, after being a very healthy person whose last visit to the hospital was to give birth, I ended up hospitalized three times in two months.

The first time was bad. I had a serious hemorrhage that worsened because of the negligence of the doctors. That day I felt the strongest pain I had in my life! It was the most unbearable physical pain I have ever experienced. Now, add the emotional pain and you will have an idea of what my dream had turned into.

I had wanted to go to Mexico City in the first place, and not Guadalajara, because I had a lot of family in Guadalajara, and I didn't want to have to explain my situation and justify my decisions. That was exactly what I was running away from. But I ended up there. And, surrounded by family, I managed to feel completely isolated.

If in that time you had looked up "introvert" in the dictionary, you would have found my face. I totally caved in.

The safety net

The hardest and most blissful lesson I learned was that human beings were not made to be alone.

Did you know that there are biological explanations for it? There are these neurons named "von Economo" which are so interesting! Scientists think these neurons could be part of what makes us human. Some studies hypothesize that they're linked to our ability to socialize and empathize.

The research began when it was found, in a study on humpback whales, that some species presented social behavior like altruism. Go to YouTube and watch the video "Was This Whale Trying to Save a Diver's Life? | National Geographic" so you can have a better idea of what I'm talking about. If so, if we have a neurological reason to interact with people, then why do we isolate ourselves?

Later we'll go deeper into the neurological reasons and talk about how applying this theory saved me.

I isolated myself because I didn't want to be justifying, over and over again, my ambitious projects to the "rational" people. I knew what they wanted. They wanted me to admit that I was crazy and to stop trying to convince others that I was right. But I needed help! I had burned my bridges back home, and returning was not an option. So I lowered my guard, looked around... and there was my family. Aunts and cousins who lived in Guadalajara. I had not seen some of them in decades.

There they were offering me any help I could need, and best of all, weren't asking questions. They were just being there for me. One by one they waved the safety net that held me until I was able to recover myself, build strong foundations, and thrive. This time not only for me and my boys, but for those who were there, and every person I love.

It is important to recognize those who helped... and just as important to be aware of those who interfere and even destroy, often without knowing it.

Save yourself first

In case of an emergency, oxygen masks will drop down in front of you. Please pull the mask down toward your face and place the mask over your mouth and nose. If you are traveling with a child, please **attend to yourself first, then the child**.

You've heard that, haven't you?

It's true everywhere! You're not going to be able to help others if you don't protect yourself first. Remember **STAnd**? That's part of protecting yourself and making better choices.

1. Stop
2. Think
3. Act

Now we're talking about people, and not an airplane losing pressure.

Von Economo neurons prompt us to socialize, but they do not protect us from the harmful actions of evil people. For that, we need to be observant and evaluate situations (Stop), acquire knowledge (Think) and experiment (Act).

Let's go deeper into Stop.
1. Stop: Evaluate the Situation
This is not an easy task, especially when you consider that the criteria will be different for each person.

> While writing this book, I was participating in an influential committee to improve education in Mexico. Among the members were leaders of the most recognized universities, businesses, and civil associations in the country. And, although we all arrived there believing that we had a clear idea of what the ideal goal of education would be, after hours of debate, I was able to see how the context and perspective of each of us, regarding education, had too many variables.
>
> Fortunately, there are also factors in common between people—similarities—and these factors are what allow progress and achievement.

In short, I have noticed that the factors in common have ethical aspects. The information on which they are based is more objective; it is measurable, accountable, and verifiable. While the common factors are ethical, and based in objectivity, the most debatable variables are always – now I dare to say it: always! – ruled by moral codes; so they are subjective, out of strict control and management and, therefore, perishable.

In a few chapters, we will talk in depth about the differences between ethics and morals. For now, it is enough to know that morality is useful and applicable in limited contexts, such as the time, place and needs of a specific group, while ethics obey a greater good for a greater number of people. Ethics transcend place, belief, race, and time.

All this is to establish a criterion to evaluate situations with a smaller margin of error. From here on, the concepts of good or bad and right or wrong will be considered according to whether they achieve success for the majority in the long term, or if their results are for a few and of a short duration.

Be aware that, in the context of this book, will be talking about situations caused by people.

I would love to tell you that evaluating a situation 100% objectively, without prejudice and without emotions, is possible. **But it makes me even happier to say it is not!**

No, it is not possible. At least not in this universe. At least not on this planet. Emotions, feelings and experiences are the most powerful forces of action we have. They are what makes us alive; they are what makes us human. But what would become of us if we depended on nothing else? Fortunately, it also makes us human to have a rational brain that allows us to be aware; to recognize impulses and emotions, and enjoy or handle them, instead of being at their mercy.

Therefore, the first step of the evaluation is to make a clear, concise, and objective list of these three points:

1. What is happening? Not judgments, the real situation as it is.
2. What should not be happening? What benefits the few or harms the majority.
3. What should be happening? What benefits the majority in the long term.

Your background
In addition to assessing the situation in general, including environments and people, it is important that you evaluate your own position.

The main obstacles to objectively assessing a situation are our own experiences.

That person who you have never met before and who, for no reason, you can't stand; that place that makes you feel restless or fearful just because; or even the sudden, random pain that you have never been able to figure out! All these have their origin in experiences which, throughout your life, have been stored somewhere in your mind as unconscious stimuli, which sabotage the possibility of correctly assessing situations.

In addition to hindering objective thinking, these reactive impulses are decisive whether you decide to take action, stay on the sidelines, or even obstruct a solution.

Each of these experiences can be localized in your mind and worked on until they cease to have negative effects on you.

Until then, being aware that this is happening, and having the basic information on how to handle the reactions you experience in your relationships with other people, will help you enormously.

Now that you have an idea of how past experiences impact the way a person makes their own judgments, think of any group of people. Now, imagine the possible number of combinations of backgrounds and impulsive reaccions in it. Then multiply it by the number of groups that form our society. Can you see now why is there such a chaos of interpersonal relationships?
The good news is that this phenomenon has been studied and patterns have been found.

To begin with, we will identify three main categories: the good, the bad, and the confused.

The good, the bad, and the confused:
Now, I will explain to you, in the easiest and most digestible way I can, what has for me been the most valuable knowledge about the human condition. Take this as the first approach to start seeing what you haven't seen before. We'll discuss it more in chapter 7.

The science behind this[3] is so fascinatingly exact that it has propelled my life in an unimaginable way.

---

[3] Science of Survival (1951) L. Ron Hubbard

The Superhero Lifestyle for Teachers

There are mainly three zones where people move:

1. Freedom and fulfillment zone
2. Confusion zone
3. Fear zone

No matter what, despite any challenge, superheroes always move towards the freedom and fulfillment zone. They are action takers, so, let's call them **the good**.

Villains live in fear. They see everything around them as something dangerous that constantly wants to destroy them, so they protect themselves by controlling or destroying these things first. They obstruct the solutions, so, let's call them **the bad**.

Everybody else is somewhere in the confusion zone, which has different levels of confusion. The closer they are to the freedom zone, the more chances they have to go up, be free, and succeed. The closer they are to the fear zone, the more susceptible they are to fail and be pray of the villains. They may be oscillating, or hidden on the sidelines, so, they'll be **the confused**.

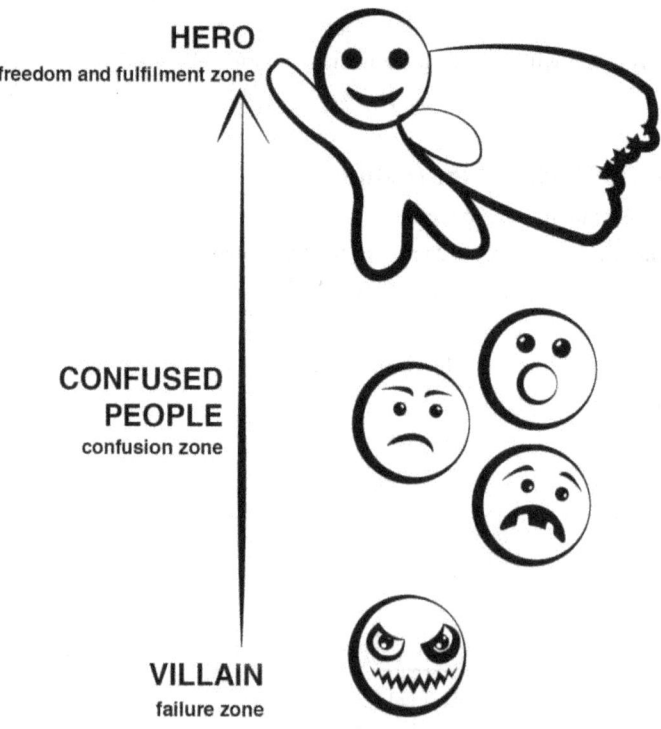

Not only the good ones have superpowers
But if you are reading this book and not "The Supervillains Lifestyle", I assume you are not the enemy.

Why choose the heroes' and not the villains' side?

Let's put it this way: the villains use their powers to pull down and destroy. The heroes use their powers to push up and create. In the middle, there are confused people who want to go up, but are constantly bombarded by wrong information, invalidation, fear, and criticism –which, by definition, is destructive (Criticism: from PIE root *krei- "to discriminate"). So, they are easy prey for the villains; and end up causing problems for the heroes and, without knowing it, for themselves.

You may think that I'm going too far with the idea of a hero. Let me tell you that according to Christopher Reeve (formerly Superman), **a hero is an ordinary individual who finds strength to persevere and endure in spite of overwhelming obstacles**. And I agree with him! And if you do too, CONGRATULATIONS! By now, not only should you know your superpower, but you just found out you are already a hero!

I've seen repeatedly that the majority of teachers are in the confusion zone. Most of them have fabulous visions and tremendous creative potential! But they are confused about what they want to do (dreams), what they can do (power), and what they are "allowed" to do (morality). The more confused they are the more maybes they have. The more maybes they have the deeper they fall into the fear zone.

Confusion: a situation in which people do not understand what is happening, what they should do, or who someone or something is. In other words, it is when people don't have all the right and pertinent data to make a decision.

2. Think

With the previous step (**Stop** and Evaluate) you already:

    a. Have a clear idea of the situation.
    b. Are aware of the influences in your mind that promt you to take action or stay on the sidelines; or obstruct the solution.
    c. Know that others can also move towards the solution, do nothing, or cause damage.

Being honest about recognizing where someone is according to these three zones is the first step towards effective education, and solving problems.

Exercise 4.1

Instructions

Think, honestly, if you mostly solve and create (Zone 1), stay aside and let others decide (Zone 2), or hinder and/or destroy (Zone 3).

    a. Place yourself in one of the zones in the Zone Action Guide Table below, and read the suggested action for you in the column "You".
    b. Place each of the other people in the situation in one of the zones and read the suggested action for them in the column "Other".
    c. Think about how those actions can be adapted to improve your life, or solve a situation.

Zone Action Guide Table

Zone	You	Other
1 Hero	**Get a mentor.** Don't do this alone. Find like minded people. The Justice League is stronger together than any of its members are on their own.	**Support him/her.** These are the people who lead by example. Even though it is, oftentimes, hard to understand them, and even harder to follow them, they are opening paths for you.

Zone	You	Other
2 Confused	**Trust your intuition.** Trust that you can recognize truth when you see it, and don't be afraid to confront it. Stay away from bad news and gossips. Go to the source when you want to learn or understand something. Take baby steps if you need to. Or giant leaps if you're ready for it. **But keep on moving forward.**	**Understand that this person is confused.** This people need to move at their own pace. **Guide them.** Give them as much information and support as you can, **but don't do things for them.** It is important for them to take action. In other words, assume your responsibility towards them, and let them assume their own.
3 Villain	There is a reason you feel that everybody else is an enemy. And there are ways to find the real enemy — the real problem — and defeat it.	Do not try to reason with them. They are the most confused of all. While you learn and gain better tools and technologies to deal with villains, you need to <u>keep your boundaries firm.</u>

3. **Act**

   a) Adapt the suggested actions of the previous table to the situation you want to solve based on the answers in step 1- Stop. Now, commit to:

       a. Firmly stopping what should not be happening.

       b. Reinforcing and/or start what should be happening.

Exercise 4.2

1. Below, in the column "You", besides the zone you think you are in now, (the one you placed yourself in a minute ago), write the specific actions that you are going to take.
2. In the column "Other", make a list of the people involved in the situation, and organize them in each of the three zones.
3. Now you know who will support you, who will stay on the sidelines, and who will try to defeat you.

Note: Keep in mind that your perception of who is in each of these areas is personal. Well, remember that your unconscious background may be influencing your decisions.

Zone	You	Other
1 Hero		
2 Confused		
3 Villain		

3 Important notes

1. I cannot emphasize enough **the importance of this knowledge**. Read through the exercise again, and answer it again. If you have left the previous exercises blank, please don't skip this one.

2. **Being an introvert is not a positive quality,** no matter how much we justify it while being one.
3. **Do not underestimate the villains.** The most dangerous are not openly bad. You'll recognize them because they seem to help you, but – in an almost mysterious way – at the end, you remain in the same place you were before, or find that things have got worse.

The best way to proceed

Let's take a closer look to the villains. Don't you feel empathy for some of them? The Joker, for example, he is awesome! How about the Grinch? Not to mention Loki or Venom. Maleficent! It is hard not to love her after the movie about her life and how she became evil after a painful betrayal.

You see where I'm going, don't you? There is a reason that villains become villains. But that doesn't mean that we have to let them do harm. If they cannot control themselves, somebody must do it. We can control them by setting firm limits. And that is as much as we can do until they get out of the fear zone, move to the confusion zone, and start moving up... if they do.

Let's clear up the fact that control does not mean making others do as we please.

> To control is the ability to start, continue, and stop an action.

Even with a desirable action, if there is no control it becomes inefficient or harmful. If you cannot start, continue, and stop it at the right time, then it will not produce the expected results. If it is an undesirable action that has already started and continues, then it must be stopped.

> Surprisingly, the best way to make someone hate us is to let them hurt us.

It seems logical and natural not to let others hurt us; but there are social protocols that have taught us to duck, endure, and try to get along with those doing the hurting; either because it is a superior, a relative, a child, or someone with some apparent disadvantage. Instead of pushing back, we submit, avoid, or delay. Give confrontation a try! Invariably, in each case when you put out a firm boundary to avoid harm, and take appropriate actions to control the situation, the aggressor goes from a state of hatred to one of respect... at the least.

Let me share an example. This actually happened in a fifth-grade class, and, with a few differences in each situation, I've seen it happen over and over.

When the the program I was running began at an elementary school in Guadalajara, Mexico, the fifth-grade teacher gave us an overview of her group:
- 38 students.
- Mostly regular and more or less quiet, not very collaborative.
- Three smart and introverted girls.
- One negative leader with no respect for his classmates or for his teacher.

The group, in general, showed ups and downs. Sometimes they advanced and participated according to what was expected. At other times they were distracted, disrespectful, and showed few results.

The main component of the program was an exercise that the whole group had to do at the beginning of class. On the first occasion it was almost impossible. The negative leader was constantly breaking everyone's concentration, and the rest of the group reacted to those disruptions - except for the introverts, who did nothing.

How did we apply **STA**nd — the Stop, Think and Act method— according to the bad, the good, and the confused?

For **Stop**, we make a clear, concise, and objective list of these three points:

1. What was happening?
    a. The group had to learn a new practice and exercise it every day.
    b. The influence of the negative leader was preventing this from happening.
    c. According to the Zone Action Guide Table, we found this:
        i. The good: no one.
        ii. The bad: the misbehaving boy.
        iii. The confused: the rest of the group and the teacher.
        Observe that, since the teacher was being dominated by the student, there was no hero to follow, so the rest of the group was fearfully reacting to this boy's action. They did not dare to act against him, because they did not think someone was looking after them. Their teacher did not represent the authority they needed to represent.

2. What should not be happening?

        a.   The misbehaving boy should not be disruptive.
        b.   The rest of the students should not react to his harmful actions.
        c.   The teacher should not allow such behavior, and should keep her calm.

3. What should be happening?
   a. The teacher must move to Zone 1 - The good - and then must take control.
   b. The rest of the group should be able to recognize the teacher's leadership, and build enough self-control to concentrate and do their exercises.
   c. The negative leader should be contained, studied, and handled appropriately.

For **Think**, analyze what to do according to where is each one in the Zone Action Guide Table.

> Teacher in Zone 2: Understand that she is confused. She needs to move at her own pace. Guide her. Give her as much information and support as you can, but don't do the things for her. It is important for her to take action. In other words, assume your responsibility towards her, and let her assume her own.
> Disruptive child in Zone 3: Do not try to reason with him. He is the most confused of all. Set and keep firm boundaries.

For **Act**, firmly stop what should not be happening and reinforce what should be happening.

> We helped the teacher find her superpowers, trust what she believed was right, and guided her to not be afraid to act accordingly. Before, she had not set firm boundaries for this child for fear of confronting his parents or other teachers.
> We were able to teach her the proper methods to control bad actions. She gained confidence until, based on the recommendations for dealing with others in Zone 3, she did not try to reason with him, but calmly and firmly taught the kid what was allowed and was not. In a way we could say that she gradually controlled him, but what really happened is that she showed him that he could control himself.

To my satisfaction, when I visited her classroom a couple of months later, it was with a tear in my eye as I witnessed how the, once bullying, boy who used to disrupt the entire class, now stood in front of the group leading a perfect and beautiful exercise!

CHAPTER 5:
THE EDGE

If you haven't seen the movie *The Edge* (1997) yet, go now and put it on top of your must-watch list. Anthony Hopkins' character is brilliant! In some ways, that character represents a lot of what we have been discussing here.

The film is about survival; there's a part of the movie where Charles (the protagonist) must either get rid of a bear, or be its prey. He knows about Native American tribes where young men are asked to kill a bear as a rite of passage into adulthood. Having that knowledge, he succeeds in hunting the bear. The whole time, Charles firmly believes that

> if one person can do it, anyone can do.

I appropriated that sentence to my own survival, to keep myself away from excuses and from playing the victim.

Being able to do anything is a process. It is not something that you just go and do. It is a **technique that needs to be mastered**. It is not like just watch someone do something, and then go and do it in your own way. It is a science; it is a process of following the exact same steps to get the exact same results.

I spent years researching the problems in the education system without finding the right answers —nearly three decades!

Then, while in India, I found part of it; a technology to improve certain functions of the brain. Visiting some of the poorest villages near Chennai, I was amazed to witness how the children using that technology stood out remarkably from other children, including their peers in more developed regions. It basically consisted of a series of exercises with sounds to activate specific parts of the brain, which results in increased intelligence; not only the kind that is measured with an IQ test, but also that natural intelligence that includes intuition, self-determinism, empathy, and communication; those soft skills that push us to higher and more transcendental goals.

Going back to my experience in India, the impact was such that from that point onward I dedicated myself to mastering the subject, and created a system to implemented it in Mexico. In six years, I shared it with more than 850 teachers and more than 24,000 students; and the numbers keep on increasing. What's important to observe here is that, invariably, when the participants apply the techniques to the letter, they get the expected results. When they don't, the constant result is a bunch of justifications and "reasons" why it doesn't work or "is not for them". When they follow the method, they succeed. When they don't, <u>they create excuses</u> about why it has not succeeded. I've observed this very same phenomena happen with all other technologies and methods that I have shared to improve something.

This chapter is about making things happen.

The biggest error we make when we are learning something new from someone else is that we do it in our own way. We think that we know better than those who are teaching us.

It is a natural process of the brain to take what's new and compare it with something we already know. And that's OK, because that gives us confidence to accept the new. What is not OK is mixing the new with the old.

Sometimes, when we teach our techniques, teachers think: "Ah! It's like musical intelligence; it's like Neurolinguistic Programming; …it's like brain gym;" …and then they start mixing it all; they don't achieve the results they expect, and then they say our tech doesn't work.

Maybe you've read a book or taken a course about being rich, being healthier, improving your relationships, or doing anything which improves your life –and didn't get the results you wanted.

Go back to that time. Review the specific steps that you should have taken. See if you followed them to the letter, or if you made short-cuts or changed or added things on your own initiative.

There will come a time when you can make things on your own way, but the old saying— "learn the rules before you go breaking them" - exists for a reason. You can modify techniques that you learn, but you have to **learn them first**. Modifying techniques without knowing the *entire* technique, even if your modifications are not *bad*, will lead to unintended consequences which could get in the way of success.

Let's do it the right way
The most misunderstood step is **Action.**
Either because it is done incorrectly, or not done at all because too much time is spent waiting to make it perfect, or waiting for the perfect time to start. Sometimes it's because actions aren't repeated long enough to achieve results.

Don't believe me? Prove it to yourself. It won't be real for you if you haven't experienced it firsthand.

1. Take one of those processes that you believed that would work for you, and which was proven to work (this is important) for others who applied it correctly.
2. Then take very specific steps from it. That is, the superior data, what's left after taking off everything that helps you understand a point. Take this very book, for example. It has stories, examples, references, and different ways to explain the same thing. All of that is necessary to open communication lines and have a better understanding of the contents. But there are exercises that ask you to take very specific actions which will lead to results. When you finish reading this book, you can always go back to the exercises only, and reach higher levels in the same aspects. Chapter 14 was made to help you with this.
3. Apply them to the letter. That means *to apply them to the letter*.
4. Take action *immediately*. Don't wait for better times.
5. Don't worry about making it perfect; focus on making it happen.
6. Continue until you get results. Don't stop until you obtain them. Do not invent "reasons" to stop!

That last step is called commitment. You do not stop until you have succeeded.
Commitment: to give in charge, entrust. From Latin *committere* "to unite, connect, combine; to bring together".

It is not enough to agree with something (that will happen when you learn how to do it) — you need to experience it! That's the only way to make it yours; and that happens by committing to do it.
In short:
1. **Gather information**: Do all the research you need. Organize your way forward in clear steps, and include execution times. Do not simply list "I will work on a chapter of this book" — set a deadline for when that chapter will be complete!

Then:

2. **Commit**: Stop asking questions. Stop searching for answers before you begin or changing steps before you start. **Just commit**. Connect every piece and make sure it works.
3. Realize it's okay to make mistakes. You will get to the end of the process with something finished, and you will see that it has some mistakes. And you will then, having done everything else, be in the position to fix them.

How I got back on my feet

First things first. I'm in the city with no support—right then, I needed shelter and income. I lived a couple of months in an aunt's house, and then I rented a small cheap room in a not so good area of the city, but at least I had a mattress on the floor and a foldable table to work on.

I made an agreement with the organization that I had been previously working with in my former city. The deal: I had to give them results in three months, in which they would keep on paying me. The problem? I had to perform the work in schools, and it was the end of July; they were on vacation until September!

> "Mom, the good thing is that you do not believe in impossible."

Rodrigo, my son, told me that before I left for Mexico. I held onto it. It became my mantra—and I went for it.

I committed to do the work, even if I needed to go to the principals' houses to speak to them. Fortunately, it was not necessary. My fairy godmother (Rosalba, my aunt) got me special appointments with three schools.

Know what? There's some kind of magic that happens when you are totally focused on one clear and specific target, and you cannot afford to get distracted by gloomy predictions, horror stories, gossip, and bad news. I had work to do, and no other option than to do it.

I was new to the city and had no prejudices. What I did have was a very tight budget. So, I looked for a room, based on what I could afford and not on how pretty and comfortable it was.

I ended up living in what, I was told later, was one of the most dangerous neighborhoods of the city. Yes, I could tell it was not the best place to live based on the people there, the kind of houses, and what surrounded them. But who cared?! All I needed was a place to stay. I made sure to be back home before it got dark, walked with my head held high, and treated anyone as if I had lived there my whole life. To be honest, I was not acting. I had my head held high, but I didn't look down on anyone. I was really thankful for them, for being there; without that neighborhood, I would not have had a place to stay.

And here I am now. Safe and sound.

In no way am I recommending doing this. It was risky and it's not something I would do again. I share this story to prevent someone else from reaching this extreme. Start *now*. Do not wait until you have no ground left to retreat to.

Also, I would not say I started from scratch, either. While I was financially bankrupt, my greatest wealth was in the knowledge and experiences that I had gained throughout my life. In other words, all those previous years, even if I had not known it then, I was building the foundations I would later use to make things happen!

It is science

It is a matter of finding the right formula and sticking to it. It's about asking yourself a few questions before you start... and then getting it done.

How do we know this is the right formula? Because it has been proven to work.

Why does that make it a science? Because every time you follow the exact same steps, you obtain the exact same results. This is not a science done in labs, under vents and in lab-coats. This is a science done in *life*.

In India I learned how to apply the brain exercises in places where the children gather after school for a couple of hours to practice them, get help with their homework, and receive life lessons.

I first replicated the exact same model in Mexico, but it didn't work. The culture was different, so I had to adapt. <<But, Lucía, you just said don't change anything!>>.

There's the trick!

Stick to the formula and adjust the details. I did not start by changing the formula. I tried it; it did not work; I kept the technology intact, isolated the steps that had –and could-- be changed; I changed them; I acted.

The brain exercises were working just fine. They were previously proven by prominent scientists and thousands of students. But the way to apply it had not been successful out of India. The application model required a new formula, but not new techniques.
That is: the form changed, but **not the essence**.

After *six years* of thorough research, experiences, success and failure, I got a formula that works like a charm!

The best thing? It not only applies to teaching brain exercises. It applies to life; it applies to any project you wish to succeed.

Formula #2: Make Things Happen

1. An ethical and clear goal

2. Logical steps to connect the goal with the foundation

3. A solid foundation

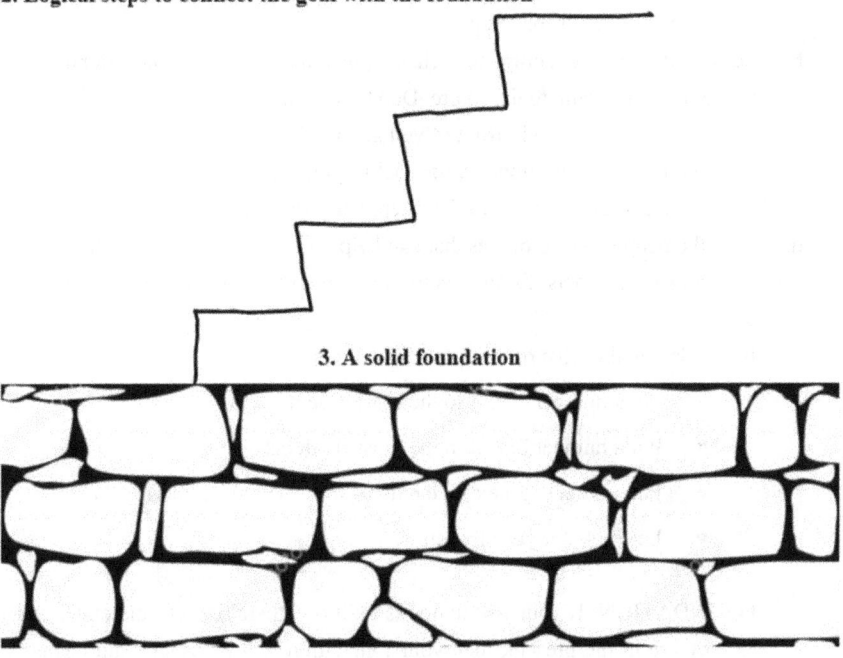

1. GOAL: Two keywords here: Ethical and Clear.

   Ethics: Rationality toward *the highest level of survival* for the individual, the future race, the group, and mankind. It is about creating the greatest amount of good for the greatest amount of people, including yourself... *mainly yourself.*

   Clear: Completely, entirely, wholly. Without ambiguities.

The more detailed and clear your plan is, the more likely it is to happen. The more ethical it is, the more satisfactory and long lasting your results will be.

2. STEPS: Here is where most people fail, because they want to eat the elephant in one bite. They want to take on the world—all at once. You have to cut it in little pieces and eat it one bite at a time.

   a. You know your end-goal. Now, reverse engineer from your goal to the present. Think backwards. Not from where you are now to where you want to be. Imagine your goal as already achieved, and think about what should have happened right before. And write it down. Now focus on that new step and think what should have happened right before that. Then, continue doing so until this very moment.
   There you are! Your roadmap!
   b. Set specific times to complete each step, then mark them in your calendar. Stay in the present, facing to the future. Don't look back.
   c. Take the very first step in front of you and totally focus on it. Forget about the rest. But continue visualizing your goal in as much detail as possible. Totally commit to achieving that very first step. Once done, take the next step.
   d. Find the people and resources that can help you achieve each step. Base your decisions in real facts; listen to your intuition, but support it with measurable data.
   e. Every day, make a list of things to do and number them:
      - Put a number 1 next to the most urgent items.
      - Put a number 2 next to the must-do items.
      - Put a number 3 next to the items that "would be good to do".
      - Leave 4s for your free time.

   4. FOUNDATION: If your foundation is built on others' beliefs and expectations as they are in the present, then your foundation will be as soft and change as

frequently as the people around you change, and the way you interpret the world changes. If it is built on your own needs and wants, your foundation will be solid because, very surely, your life will depend on it.

You are not putting your life at risk to succeed... but you are making sure to succeed in such a way that your life *will not be at risk*. Here, and only here, is where your superpowers activate... and when they're active, you can put them to work so they get stronger. Because as you move forward, the naysayers will try harder to stop you. And you should be strong enough **to be you...** and not let the naysayers succeed.

This is the longest and most difficult stage. It is a constant formation throughout your life. When you look forward, it seems that there is still much to learn... but when you turn back and recognize your achievements, you know what you have gained and have experience that will support you.

You should know that you do not have to wait until it is completely finished. You can look back every few steps and see everything you have accomplished. And your ability to be strong enough **to be you** will continue to be reinforced as you build steps towards your goal.

This formula to make things happen is the closest thing I've found to a magic wand. Are you also a fan of Harry Potter? Because that's the kind of magic wand I'm talking about.

> Harry had waved what felt like every wand in the shop, until at last he had found the one that suited him — this one, which was made of holly, eleven inches long, and contained a single feather from the tail of a phoenix. Mr. Ollivander had been very surprised that Harry had been so compatible with this wand. "Curious," he had said, "curious," and not until Harry asked what was curious had Mr Ollivander explained that the phoenix feather in Harry's wand had come from the same bird that had supplied the core of Lord Voldemort's.
>
> —Description of Harry's wand[4]

Harry's wand is unique for him. It has THE core essence (foundation) that Harry needs to achieve his goal (his ethical goal): defeat Lord Voldemort. But of course, the wand does not act by itself; Harry had to learn how to use it. He had to have teachers, mentors; learn spells... learn to believe in himself.

---

[4] https://harrypotter.fandom.com/wiki/Harry_Potter%27s_wand

Exercise 5.1: Your magic wand

Follow the instructions in each column. Feel free to make adjustments to the answers of your missions as you move forward. If you haven't done Exercises 1, 2, and 3, you might want to go back and do those first.

FOUNDATION	GOAL
1. Write the problem that you stated in Exercise 1. Write down if it only affects you, or if it also affects others. 2. Write how your superpowers (from Exercise 2.2) can help you solve it. 3. What other knowledge, experiences and abilities form your core essence?	Go back to the first exercise, and envision a world in which that problem is already solved. Try making that your goal, and describe it in as much detail as you can. Use the work sheet below to help you do this.

Exercise 5.2: Your magic wand II

	The steps
1. Imagine your goal as already complete and write every step from your goal to present time (apply reverse engineering). Use your imagination.	Goal _____ Steps ○ ○ ○ ○ ○ ○○
2. Set specific deadlines for each step to be fulfilled, then mark them in your calendar. Don't worry about reasonable details here. Use your imagination.	○ ○ ○ ○ ○ ○ ○
3. Take the last step from list 1 and describe it in as much detail as possible.	
4. Commit to making that step happen.	Describe exactly what you need to do. ○ ○ ○ ○ ○ ○ ○

CHAPTER 6: AUTHORITY

One of the first things you learn in school is to obey authority.

You learn that authority should never be questioned – much less challenged.

> Recently, I attended a presentation by the board of a group of "defenders" of teachers. That group was created in the early 80s. To my surprise, after almost 4 decades, they seem to be fighting the same fights they started back then!

In a way, it made sense when I found out that everybody in the board changed every certain time, but one: the founder president.

He was the higher authority who would always have the final word. He seemed to be trapped in the past. It was not only how he spoke, but his whole appearance took me back in time. It was said by his presenter that one of his main qualities was persistence. That he had held on for all those years and would continue doing so for as long as needed because, someday, that persistence would yield victory!

The hall talks were different. The newest generations expressed a desire for a different direction, but seemed resigned to the fact that nothing would change. Because there was no way to change things in that group – which, by the way, had strong political power – while the head was a president for life who would never understand them.

Insanity

Insanity is doing the same thing over and over again, and expecting to achieve different results.

Time has proven that war does not end war. Fighting against what we do not want is a way of reinforcing what we do not want. But still, here we are as humanity fighting against corruption, fighting against criminals, fighting against diseases, and fighting against poor educational systems.

Am I suggesting we just let them be?! NO.

Go back to the good, the bad, and the confused lesson from Chapter 4. That's what I am suggesting.

What if instead of fighting pollution, we created sustainable ecosystems?

What if instead of fighting criminals, we healed their brains and helped them reintegrate into society?

What if instead of spending millions in understanding diseases, that money was used in understanding health and making it a lifestyle?

What if instead of fighting poor educational systems, we reinforced and expanded the good ones?

Of course, these questions are not the final questions. There are so many of them! But they show that we want to reframe how we think about solving problems.

We could make the world better by focusing on *creating good* systems instead of *fighting bad* ones. There are proven examples already happening around the world!
The strongest obstacles for those making things happen are the people in the lowest stages of the confusion zone. Those confused people are the most likely to keep doing the same thing, and then waiting for something different to happen. The saddest part of this is that many people in the highest stages of the confusion zone — nearly at the freedom and fulfilment zone — can get easily trapped in the emotional dramas of the confused ones. They get stuck trying to help those more confused people, while having neither the right information nor the right tools to do so.

Often getting the right tools and correct information, and put it to good use, requires skill. Are you ready to talk more about authority?

Authority
Authority: the moral or legal right or ability to control. From the Latin auctoritatem (nominative auctoritas) "invention, advice, opinion, influence, command," from auctor "master, leader, author" with "power derived from good reputation; power to convince people, capacity for inspiring trust."

According to this, authority should be something earned from a good reputation, a power to convince people, or a capacity to inspire trust. But this is not the definition that we learn in our early years. We learn by experience that it is mostly arbitrarily assigned and that we cannot do anything about it. So, we grow up with some frustration and resentment toward authority.

The good news is that when it is gained through good leadership and derived from knowledge and results, authority becomes something to respect.

> The main difference between one
> and the other is the level of responsibility.

Understanding responsibility as an ability to respond to a situation is important to give correct answers and achieve positive results.

For instance, pretend you are in school and have two teachers. One of these two has better prepared classes than the other. Let's imagine that the less prepared one is the principal's favorite, and so he is assigned the authority to take the place of the director when the principal is not there. One of those days, an angry mother arrives asking for explanations for what she considers an unfair action from a teacher to her son.

The teacher with "authority" gets scared and does not know what to do. He *cannot respond* to the situation. He says that she must wait for the principal to come back. But she does not want to wait. She demands an immediate response.

The other teacher — the better prepared teacher —is notified of the problem *and comes to help* (he responds). He analyzes the situation, gathers the pertinent facts, focuses on the problem – not on the people – and finds the solution.

Now who do you think is the highest authority?

Authority	
Earned	**Arbitrarily assigned**
Takes time	Imposed
Manages control	Imposes control
Serves others	Serves itself
Recognized by others	Feared by others
Responsible	Irresponsible

Be the authority in your space… then expand your space

To get back on my feet I had to have something or someone to hold on and make sure it would remain steady. First, I thought it would be enough to hold onto my beliefs and on myself. The funny thing is that what we believe is not always what what actually happened. If we have been hurt, we believe that certain path, action, *or person* is not good, when very likely it was not that path, action, or person that hurt us, but the way we perceived it, and the decisions and actions resulting from our perception and judgment about it.

Sure, I was making radical changes! But I was not having the expected results. Then, surely, there was something that I was missing.

I really believed I had changed everything! How come I was not having different results?!

…I had changed *almost* everything. As the good introvert I was, I had almost proudly avoided social interaction. My decisions and actions were being based on painful (emotional) perceptions and, therefore, irrational judgments.

Have you ever met an introverted baby? Of course not! No one is born an introvert. A baby cries for food, for attention, for help, and for whatever he needs and wants.

Introversion is learned, as we grow and begin to be scolded, limited, and criticized for things we do not understand. We begin to retract; we avoid any socialization because we don't understand others and we are sure they don't understand us either. Cautiously, we pick a few people who seem to resonate with us, and we learn diplomacy to survive as a human being.

It had its perks. I was (and still am) the highest authority in Lucyland. There's where I got to create my big visions. But, out in the rest of the world, God! It was more about fighting barriers than making dreams come true.

It was when I opened myself to new points of view that I could see things as they were and not as I thought they "should be". Being able to see things without pain, fear, or anger opened me to an amazing new perspective and, therefore, a safe and interesting entrance gate to extroversion.

The steady support that finally lifted me up was the right data, and the right mentor.

Find your Yoda, or better yet, your Yodas

This is where I tell you that you need a Yoda in your life. Not a friend or someone to comfort you. But *someone who has already achieved what you want*. Someone who will speak straight and tell you what you need to know, not what you want to hear... sometimes, you won't know until it's too late. If you're lucky, you will realize it before they leave your life.

It is not always fun, but as you move forward, breaking barriers is indescribably rewarding. If you are skeptical about needing a Yoda — needing a mentor — that might be a barrier you have to break. You must, because you cannot go forward alone... and you may miss a lot of education —real, human education from a mentor — if you refuse to believe you need one.

Be aware that you will not have only one Yoda. You will have different mentors throughout your life. Or one Yoda in different disguises, if you like.

Yoda was an outstanding Jedi master. 900 years of experience and knowledge gave him the wisdom and force to make him one of the most powerful defenders of peace in the galaxy. He even unlocked the path to immortality. That is not only having authority: it is *being* authority. If you want to be a Jedi, you know who to look for.

You may not want to be a Jedi. Let's consider that many people's dreams are modest, and that's perfectly fine! In those cases, you will not go after the most outstanding master, but the one who will guide you to where you want to go... even if you are not totally clear where to go just yet. Just train your eyes to see what you like, and focus on what strengthens your power –remember to focus on building the good instead of fighting the bad. Eventually, you will find environments, information, or people who represent or have what you want for yourself. Those are your first mentors! As you move forward you will find some more specialized.

> I met a second-grade teacher who worked double shifts. That was fine until her first baby was born. She wanted to spend more time with her daughter, but she also needed the income she had from the two shifts in different schools. Among the options she considered, she thought about giving private lessons at home in the afternoons. So she found a teacher who was already doing that. When she asked him for advice, he gladly gave it to her.

This is something interesting. I have seen dozens of people afraid to ask for help, while they themselves, happily, would respond to the request of someone else. Most people are willing to help. Do not hesitate to ask. And if you get a no for an answer, it's okay; go to option B or C, D… and as many as it takes. Always remember to keep your eyes on your north star, and not on the cliffs, swells, and storms that may appear in your path.

I've been fortunate to find a mentor who helps me remain ethical. **And that's gold!**

That's the way I realized—at last—that it was about awareness and responsibility. It was about building authority in a wider range of areas:
1. Myself
2. My nuclear family and my direct creations
3. My work, my friends, and colleagues
4. My direct or indirect influence on all humankind

It was about knowing that life doesn't happen to you. It happens from you and because of you. As I said before, if my life and destiny were written, I was the author! So I could rewrite it at will.

That was the missing piece in my foundation that was not leading me toward *my* goal! It was *my* goal, not someone else's. How could somebody else have a higher authority in it?

You are the author of your own goal!
You write your own screenplay and you dictate the rules of your own life. But there may be someone who has gotten further than you who can help you. So, the game here is to protect our self-determinism from negative influences, while being open to the right guidance.

Now that you are aware that your goal is yours, and *you* get to decide what to do with it, you are ready to share it and not be afraid of doing so. Because you're going to choose carefully who to share it with, and why you are sharing it.

My advice is to share it first with whoever is going to help you achieve it. Keep it away from naysayers. Let them find out from your results.

Of course, the first person you want to share your goal with is your mentor. Keep in mind that good mentors are people who have already paid the price. So, you don't just go and ask them what's wrong with your life and wait for them to fix it. That is not how it works.
The two best ways I have found to get the most out of a mentor are:

1. Do your homework first.
2. Really. Do your homework first.

First, be clear on what you want *before* you reach out. Every exercise you've done, and will do in this book, is helping you to be clear, take action, and get results. Your mentor is not going to assign tasks to you; he *will* share knowledge and experience. It is you who first needs to know exactly what you want and how a mentor can help you. Do as much as possible on your own, gather all the data you can process, and take notes of all the gaps and blanks; that's the way you leverage a mentor's help.

In Exercise 5.1 you already started your homework. You set the basis to act.

In Exercise 5.2, list 4, you described what you needed to do to take the steps to make it happen.

It is time to ask yourself:

Who can help me with this?

Yes, the question is who. Not how. It is not "how I am going to make it," but "who can help me do it?"

Exercise 6: Your Yoda

1. Research everything necessary about what you are trying to achieve. But do not spend too much time on it. Search for about five different sources. Find what they have in common. Find what the basic principles are and write them down.

-
-
-
-
-

2. Number your list by priority. For each number, starting with number 1, make a list of what you need to do to make it happen. Then do it again for number 2, number 3, and the rest.

3. Name one person that can help you with it. Then write another two names just in case.
_____

4. Pretend they are sitting in front of you. What are you going to ask them?
_____

5. You have the questions. Now speak to them. Set an appointment. Write down the date and time.
_____

PART II
THE STEPS

CHAPTER 7:
ARITHM-ETHIC

— It's him! On a spider's web!

And, a short distance away...

– My fault — all my fault! If only I had stopped him when I could have! But I didn't— and now — Uncle Ben - is dead...

And a lean, silent figure slowly fades into the gathering darkness, aware at last that in this world, with a great power there must also come—great responsibility!

And so a legend is born and a new name is added to the roster of those who make the world of fantasy the most exciting realm of all!

The Spider-Man, 1962.

Minutes before, Peter Parker was excited about his new powers... unaware that they would carry dire ethical and moral conflicts. He stopped the murderer — and realized that he had let the murderer go earlier that day. Peter's inaction led to his Uncle Ben's murder!

Some superheroes have the theme where power is more of a burden than a gift. The person behind the hero is burdened by the knowledge of their powers. When Peter Parker is Spiderman, he is an extrovert; he is funny and has no limits! But when he's Peter Parker, he is a poor introvert, and cannot be with the woman he loves.
On the other hand, look at Captain America; an extroverted super-soldier who would not hesitate if he had to choose between saving one life – even his own life, or a friend's life! – or a whole city. He is smart and has a good sense of self. His personality remains the same with or without his superhero costume and shield.

There is no doubt why he is one of the mightiest Avengers and, for many, is considered a role model.

Who do you think is ethical, and who is moral?

Ethic: from Greek (hē) ēthikē (tekhnē) '(the science of) morals.

The science of morals!

Science: a systematically organized body of knowledge on a particular subject.

It's awesome! Isn't it?!

...or am I the only nerd here?

Even after four years of philosophy, I didn't realize that ethics and morals were different things. Even dictionaries still use ethics and morals as the same thing, but they are not! The word 'moral' seems to share a Proto-Indo-European root with the English word mood, which is an emotional condition, a state of mind as regards passion or feeling. It is absolutely subjective, and obeys the beliefs and feelings of certain groups, places, and times. Which is fine! Because it helps regulate social behavior for the good of the majority.

The problem with the moral codes is that they do not adapt to change. Therefore, when circumstances change but moral codes remain the same, those moral codes become problems. In fact, out-of-date moral codes are a huge problem for societies and human social circles.

It is so common that we don't notice it. But think about this: when we were young, our parents told us not to talk to strangers. And they were so strict about it! They even told us horror stories. So: we grow up (time changes), and still don't talk to strangers, and we have a terrible time trying to network, make friends, or have any sort of romantic relationship. The moral code we were taught may have worked when we were children, but once circumstances change — time, in this case — it ceases to be useful, and becomes a problem.

When we analyze a moral code to make sure that it fulfills its function, and if needed, change it to ensure that it *does* fulfill its function, it becomes ethical. Then it transcends time. Ethics is natural in human beings, and is independent of cultures and beliefs. It is measurable and can be evaluated objectively.

How can it be measured? By the amount of progress you achieve as a result of every action you take when pursuing a goal. Either as an individual or as part of a group. When you take action in pursuit of a goal, things change! That's how you can measure your ethics —how much positive change do you make during the pursuit of that goal?

Progress: from pro "forward" and gradi "to step, walk[5].

When we talk about progress, we talk about steps forward, with each step taking us closer to our goal. Here is when the main steps from the Formula to Make Things Happen are divided into smaller and smaller steps until they become everyday actions —like habits!

We have been educated, and we have educated ourselves, on foundations mostly based on moral codes. Therefore, it can be confusing to distinguish whether our actions are based on ethical or on moral principles. To solve that confusion, we went through Chapter 6 together, and saw that determining this is as simple as analyzing how much benefit or harm an action causes to the groups you can influence.

It is essential to be aware, and able to confront, that an action that benefits most of your spheres of influence can be detrimental to one or more of your other spheres. Sometimes, we decide not to do something good because it might harm a small group, and we wish to protect everyone and everything. That's insane! In the long term, we end up hurting ourselves and others more for not having carried out that action. Worst of all is how we hurt ourselves even more by feeling guilty for taking or not taking an action, and unconsciously, we begin to feel the need to constantly justify ourselves. These situations create a mental load that, gradually, deteriorates our capacities and limits our creativity.

The more aware we are of the difference between an ethical and moral action, and the more we base our actions on that distinction, the stronger our capacities get; the more our minds expand, and the more our creativity blossoms.

How to apply it in our everyday life

My moral codes told me that I had to help those in need, and that I should help everyone; that there had to be equity. Therefore, I did not move towards my goals because I felt guilty if I had something while others had nothing, or if an action I took, which was

---

[5] https://www.etymonline.com/search?q=progress

better for many people and myself, caused a slight inconvenience to someone else. I could not allow myself to be happy when others were unhappy, and could not allow myself to cause happiness in some people if it would make others unhappy. And –pay attention here– because I spent a lot of time trying to help *people who were not willing to receive help.*

How could someone not want to receive help?! Well, that could be because they didn't ask for it; or because they asked, but they did not really want to solve their problem. They only wanted attention and to keep you engaged with them.

Later I learned that people communicate differently, mostly because of their place in the 3 Zones Chart; remember that? Yes! The good, the bad, and the confused. Therefore, if I really want to help anyone, I should first find out in which zone they are in; then communicate according to the actions recommended in the Zone Action Guide Table. Doing that, I had been able to make sure that they are open to receiving the help and making good use of it.

> Remember the rule: Help yourself first.

It wasn't until I learned to help myself first, and until I recognized who I could count on, that I finally started moving forward and *progressing* at a steady pace. My life became better, I became happier, and I was able to do more good.

By applying the Arithm-Ethic Formula below, I have been able to make better decisions that have resulted in permanent improvements for myself and for others.

Formula #3: Arithm-Ethics

> The level of **Ethics** is directly proportional to the level of **Progress you achieve**, starting with **Yourself, and then** the collective group in which you exist, while you maintain your **Personal integrity**.

Pay attention to the keywords. This is all about you. It is you who builds your own **you** —**with integrity!** - so that you can grow and succeed. It is never about others. You interact with others and are influenced by them, or they're influenced by you, but in the end it's always on **you** to improve yourself.

Observe the image:

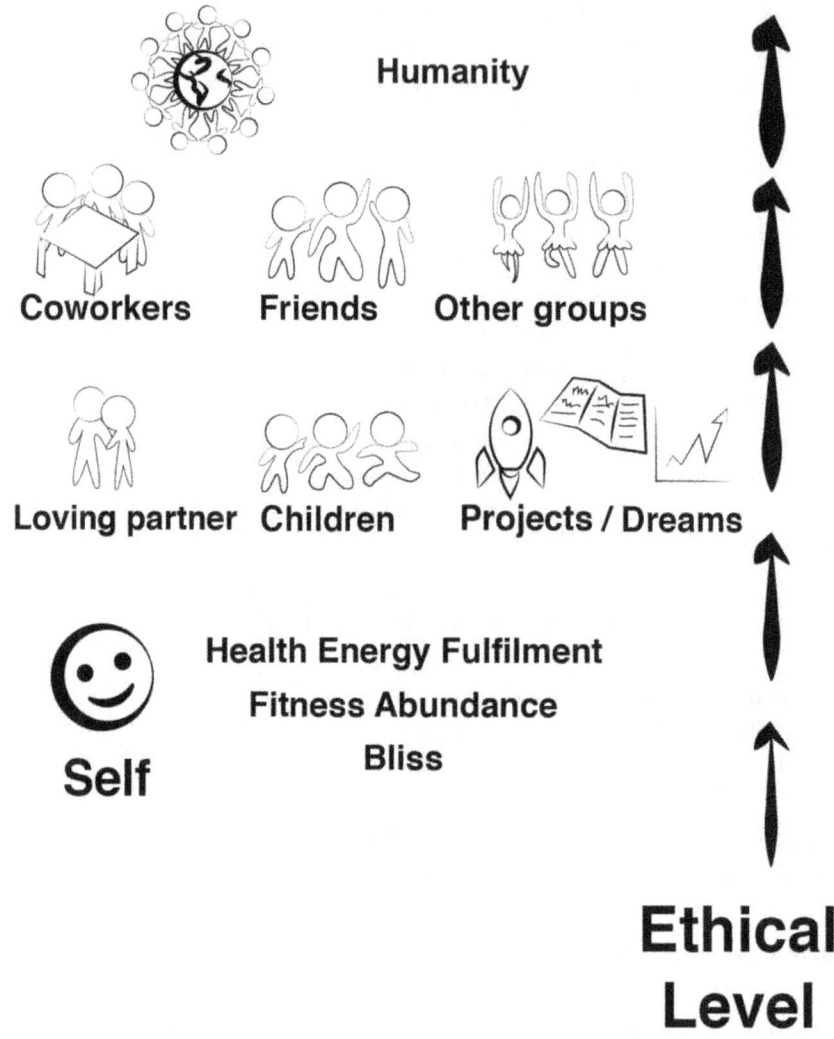

These are our main areas of action. Everything that we do, or sometimes what we stop doing, affects them in different ways.

For instance, if I dispose of my trash properly, it will avoid contaminating my house with garbage and will help protect the environment; that will have a good effect on both myself and humankind. If I eat healthy food it will benefit me, but it won't cause a direct benefit to any of the other areas. But *because* it benefits me, it will help me work through those other areas (Don't worry —if you're uncertain what every 'area' might be and need a breakdown, we're getting there!).

On another hand, if I have a team I must work with at my job —and I hate working with a team! — it will affect my production, and therefore my income, and therefore my social life, and my family life and, very surely, my health. That means it will affect three of the four areas: myself (Level 1), my partner, children, and dreams (Level 2); and my social groups (Level 3).

As hard as it may seem at first, it all starts with you. Being aware of this is the first step to success. It may be hard but let me tell you – the other way around is impossible!

The hardest part is not knowing the game, and not knowing its formulas, rules, shortcuts, tricks; and, of course, not knowing the other players.

Let's go back to the formula. Simple arithmetic; adding, subtracting, multiplying, and dividing:

1. The level of ethics is directly proportional to the level of progress (*add* levels as you reinforce yourself).
2. The progress starts with the individual (*subtract* the individual from the group, and focus on the individual).
3. The progress then expands to a wider range: to the group (*multiply* the benefits).
4. The individual maintains his personal integrity (*divide*... and rule!).

1. The level of ethics is directly proportional to the level of progress (*add* levels as you reinforce yourself).

You cannot give what you don't have. Simple logic. *Burnout is the direct result of overlooking this principle.*

Observe the formula. There is a logical reason to starting with yourself. It is not about selfishness. It is about your own survival and progress, and how ensuring your own success can help you to help others.

Think of all those teachers who have given themselves completely to their professions (Level 3) with the hope of contributing something to the creation of a better world (Level 4). On the way, they sacrifice valuable time with their family, and personal dreams and projects (Level 2). At the end, they are so tired and frustrated that they do not take care of themselves, and will become sick and suffer for it (Level 1).

How are *you* doing?

Use the following exercise to find out.

The previous chart shows only four levels; however, our actions affect more than human beings. Let's take the bigger picture, and think about our interactions with all living beings, and the material world, and your own spirituality.

Exercise 7.1: Your levels of progress

On a scale of 1 to 10, write the number that best represents your progress in each area.
1. Yourself (Health, energy, fitness, abundance, fulfilment, bliss) ____
2. Your mate, children, projects and dreams (creation and transcendence) ____
3. Your groups (at work, friends, social/development) ____
4. Your contribution to humanity (social work, charity, creation, innovation) ____
5. Your interaction with other living beings (animals, plants and nature in general) ____
6. The care of your belongings and your material environment ____
7. Your spirituality ____

Now, below, put dots in the corresponding intersections, according to the numbers, and connect them from 1 to 7.

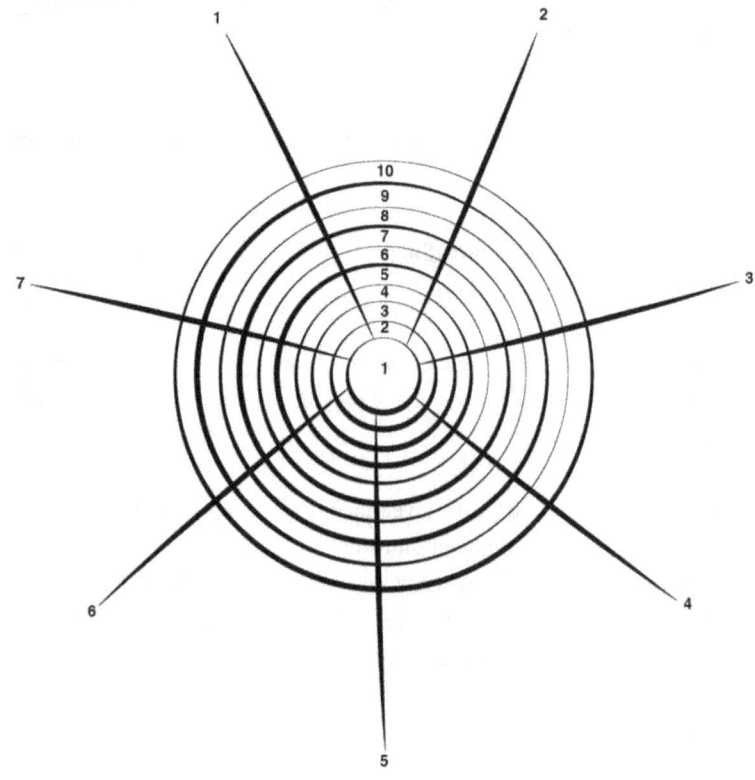

If that circle were a tire on your bike, would your ride be smooth?

Balance is important. Life is not about focusing on a particular area and forgetting all others. You will see that reinforcing one area will benefit the others, as long as the first one you reinforce is yourself.

2. The progress starts with the individual (*subtract* the individual from the group, and focus on the individual).

You will be amazed how the people in our lives influence us —it can be so hard to just be *ourselves!* Later, we are going to go deeper into this. For now, let's get rid of the louder noise: the merchants of chaos.

They are everywhere! You can find them openly dramatizing everything or covertly giving us advice for "our own good".

Here are the people in the news sharing their worst findings, disguised as good things for us to know. A few days ago, I visited a friend who always has the TV on. I was amazed to see that almost every commercial was about medication for diseases that might not even be diseases. Either those commercials are taking for granted that we all have a disease, or they are sending a subtle message that it is normal to be ill. Also, I have to say it; here is where many of our close friends are –even our loved ones! – who are always worried, telling us to do or not to do this or that, because they know best and are trying to protect us. Do they really know what's best?

I still have relatives who think that I made a mistake by not being a regular teacher in a government school. That path had "worked" for them, because it fit their beliefs and their reality, so they insisted that I should have taken their same path. A way they tried to convince me was to invalidate my decisions and to predict a terrible future if I didn't change my mind. Believe me; it's not worth the energy you spend trying to convince them otherwise.

Paying attention to all of this negativity will only take you down. In order to go up,
you must cut it off.

Exercise 7.2: Subtract to multiply
Commit yourself to not watching or listening to newscasts for two weeks. During that

time, also avoid any negative conversations and gossips. If you happen to be in a place where you cannot avoid negativity, like in some social meetings, just do not engage in it and try to change the subject as much as possible, or move away. It also may be fun to observe the game, choosing to be an objective witness. This exercise is about cleansing yourself from negative influences, so that you *can be yourself again*.

1. Fill the blanks:

I [name]_____ commit to not engage with people who drain my energy, not to watch nor listen to newscasts, nor listen to gossip and any negative conversation, from [starting date] _____to [end date] _____

2. After the end date, listen to those people again, and watch or listen to newscasts – do it! – and write down your experience and thoughts.

3. The progress expands to a wider range to the group (*multiply* the benefits).

What was the most beneficial part of your education?

Was it when an instructor just took a book out and dictated the lesson? Or was it when he took the lesson out of the book, matched it with an experience of his own, and shared it with his own words; using the book as a *guide* to make sure to cover the subject completely?

I bet we agreed on the answer.

The first option is common. The second is called *sharing*; it is called *transmitting*!

When you force yourself to do something that you don't like, or don't feel fully prepared for, then you just pass to your students what you are told. You read from the book, but you do not transmit the information —you don't make it something they can understand in real, human terms.

But, when you've found real bliss in what you do, and have the effective tools to do it and maintain it, you will not want to keep it to yourself! In fact, *it will naturally come out from you!*

> When you focus on cultivating the best in yourself,
> it will naturally expand to others.

What is it that you have transmitted to others?

There are things about you that others recognize or admire, and that you do not realize. Maybe because you believe that what you are doing is what you *have* to do, and deserve no credit; or maybe you strive so much to improve yourself that you do not recognize what you have already achieved.

Let's find out.

Exercise 7.3: Expansion is a natural tendency.
This is something I did as part of a Leadership in Innovation MIT certificate. It can be a very difficult exercise for some –as it was for me. It will also be one of the most important and rewarding. Make sure to do it to experience one of the biggest breakthroughs that you're going to have in this journey.

1. Write the names of 3 to 10 people who can give you honest information about what you stand for. Include people from work, your family, and your friends.

1 _____
2 _____
3 _____
4 _____
5 _____
6 _____
7 _____
8 _____
9 _____
10 _____

2. Ask each person to provide stories about strengths that they see in you. They have to be short. One sentence is enough. Present them this task as part of a course to improve

yourself as a teacher.

3. Gather at least 30 stories. The greater the number of stories you get, the better the results will be. Give, at the most, one week to collect the stories.

4. Make a list of the strengths common throughout those stories.
-
-
-
-
-
-
-
-
-
-

5. Circle the ones that match what you identified as your superpowers.

For some – as happened to me at the beginning – this can be an uncomfortable task. But I encourage you to do it. Get out of your comfort zone. You'll be surprised!

4. The individual maintains his personal integrity (*divide*... and rule!).
Wait... What?!

Aren't *integrity* and *division* opposites? Indeed, they are.

In order to understand the whole, you need to know its parts. You are a whole as an individual, but in the same way that a tree is a whole, when you know its different elements —such as the leaves, branches, and roots — and also know of its external influences —earth, water, and air — then you can handle them in a way that will obtain the best results.

From the many elements that make us human, let's create three main 'allies': internal parts of ourselves which are good. From the many influences of our environment, let's be aware of three main enemies: external forces that represent obstacles.

Exercise 7.4: Allies and enemies
1. Look up in a dictionary each of the words in italics, and make sure you fully under-

stand each of them.

2. Write how you could use these as *powers, or allies*:
Your *mind*

___

Your *spirit*

___

Your *willingness*

___

3. Write how these could be *obstacles, or enemies*:
Learning barriers

___

Antagonism

___

Lack of *resources* (time, money, data, tools, mentoring, teams)

___

CHAPTER 8:
"GADGETS" AND KRYPTONITE

I couldn't sleep the first time I had to withdraw the program from a school. Literally, could not sleep. I had the feeling that I had failed the students and the teachers.

When they started the program, two years before, we all knew that it would be hard. The school was in a challenging neighborhood where students' most basic needs were not met –many of them didn't have supportive families. The students were reluctant at first, but as they continued practicing the techniques, they showed improvement. This was particularly noticeable in the groups where the practice was done consistently.

Sadly, it was not reluctant students, but reluctant teachers –who were not committed to the practices– who became a bad influence for the other teachers involved and, eventually, for the students.

I was so convinced that this program was good for them that I made myself responsible for keeping them moving forward. I had the firm idea that once they saw the positive results they would crave more. But it was not like that.

At the end, only two out of nine teachers were doing the exercises. This was a public school receiving the benefits from a charitable foundation. The policy was to give them the program at no cost, but required them to commit to it. It had to be withdrawn.

It took me days to find the words and the courage to do it. They were very bad days where I was still looking for ways to fix it, trying to find out what I thought *I had done wrong*. I blamed myself and considered quitting, so that I could never fail a school like this again.

On the other hand, I wasn't financially stable yet; losing one school meant lowering my income. But it didn't feel right to keep the school because of this.

I finally did it. I explained the situation to the principal and the teachers, and withdrew the program from the school. Guess what? They didn't give a damn!

And, funny thing, right after letting that school go, *more* schools began to request the program.

Kryptonite

Every superhero can be weakened. To avoid losing your powers, you need to be very careful of the following:

1. Learning barriers
2. Antagonism
3. Lack of resources (time, money, right data, right tools, right mentoring, right team)

What happened in that school? I wasn't aware of the most important aspect of the situation: the lack of teacher motivation. I had yet to learn that while all problems can be solved, not all people want to solve their problems.

Believe it or not, having problems can be quite convenient for some people. It relieves them from responsibility and imposes the burden of the problem on others.

The strongest kryptonite: trying to help someone that doesn't want to be helped.

However, at school, we don´t get to choose who to help and who not to. Sometimes we have to confront rebel students and rude parents —not to mention antagonizing colleagues. Recall a time when you knew how to help one of them —student, parent, colleague—, and you really tried, but he or she didn't let you do it; or maybe they pretended to accept your help, which then made the problem worse, or maybe even made a new one. How energized did you feel? Didn't you feel like you were being drained? That's pure kryptonite!

And yes, I *had* to learn that.

I *had to* because I was convinced that it was always good to help; and, mistakenly, that every person would happily receive the help I offered. But, for people in the lower stages of the confusion zone, the help is seen as an insult. For them, it sends a message of "I can do something that you can't. Therefore, I'm better than you." This is why those who need help the most are often the most difficult to help. Truth be told, if you know something the other person doesn't, you are stronger in that particular aspect. People in the higher stages of the three zones understand that, and appreciate a helping hand.

When I opened myself up to new viewpoints, and when I accepted that it is okay not to save the world, and okay knowing that I could *not* save the whole world, I learned that I could protect myself from that kind of kryptonite. Even if I was sold on the moral idea of being of service to anyone "less fortunate" than me, I could choose to save myself first.

But, as I said, in the educational environment, our job is to improve our students' lives; and that implies helping them. Well, here is where our gadgets enter the game. But first, let's talk about a couple more forms of kryptonite.

A hidden type of kryptonite: to stop learning.
I thought I knew all about improving other people's lives. I was wrong.

There is a part of our human nature that drives us to believe that we know more than we really know. In a way this is useful, because if we were aware of our ignorance about the infinity of things to know, we would feel quite overwhelmed and incapable.

On the other hand, believing that we know everything that can be known about a subject inhibits our ability to learn more.

It is quite common to be in an interesting lecture or course, and to start thinking that we already know this and that; or that this or that other person we know should be learning it instead of us. It is very easy to think in terms of what other people lack. But those people lack what they lack, and if they do not want that, then every minute spent thinking about them is a minute you have wasted.

If we are unaware that we don't know about something —especially when we think we know everything— then we do not have the openness to receive new knowledge and, when someone tries to teach us, we will not take advantage of it. We may even take offense!

In the field of education this is especially important, because with so many changes, options, and implementations –many of them unsuccessful– we have reached a point where it is difficult to believe in something new.

A classmate during my philosophy career once told me "there's nothing new under the sun; everything that's worth saying has already been said." Is it right? Was it right?
Let's pretend there's nothing new. Like a fridge full of the same food every day. How many combinations could you still make?

Let's pretend everything that's worth saying had been said. Was it said in a way that everyone – no exceptions; I mean **everyone!** — would understand?

As teachers, we have a tremendously big arena to try our own combinations and communications in! The more we learn from others' successes and failures, the less susceptible to this kind of kryptonite we will be. As we learn more from what other people accomplish or attempt, we become more *accepting* of the fact that we do not know everything... and become more open to change.

An understood type of kryptonite: lack of resources.

"Heroes" like Robin Hood programmed our subconscious to think that it is bad for one person to live an abundant life while others struggle to cover their basic needs. Well, Robin Hood is just a little example of a wrong idea that we received as children and that now we pass to our students. Of course there are rich people who are bad... just as there are poor people who are bad. There are also rich people doing good things, and poor people doing good things! It is not just what we have which makes us good or bad.

We live in an abundant world, with plenty of resources for everyone. False beliefs, and a large number of confused people, are what keep us from achieving our goals.

In chapter 7, we already talked about resources such as time, money, correct data, good tools, proper mentoring, and the right team.

Until now, what's been stopping you from reaching the goal you stated in Exercise 5.1? Was it time? Money? Lack of knowledge? People?

A better way to look at this: reverse engineering. What would you be doing if you had every resource you needed, in abundance?

Exercise 8.1: Creating in abundance.

Write or draw, in as much detail as possible: what would you be doing if you had every resource you needed, in abundance?

Now, compare this vision with your goal in Exercise 5.1 (Chapter 5), and, if needed, make adjustments to the first goal according to what you have learned so far.

3 Main Gadgets
Here comes the good stuff!

You already discovered your superpower and designed your new style. It is time to get your gadgets ready!

1. An armor and a weapon
Let's start with what's going to protect you from antagonism: armor and a weapon... like the Black Panther's Vibranium Suit, and Wonder Woman's Lasso of Truth.

Armor: Special Vibranium Suit
You are not going to start the fight. But you have gotta be protected when you're attacked. Tailor your Vibranium suit alloying STAnd (Chapter 4) and the Ethics and Control formulas (Chapter 7 and 11) to overcome the effects of the "don't help me" kryptonite, and then reinforce it with a protective covering of *healthy value exchange*.

How to prepare the protective covering of *healthy value exchange*
There seems to be a natural giving-receiving law governing this universe's flows. Some giving-receiving exchanges are immediate, while others are mediated by one or more actors. For instance, you plant a seed, take good care of the plant, and receive a good fruit (immediate). Or you plant a seed in a good place and forget about it; the soil, sun, and rain do their jobs; the seed grows and gives fruit, which is eaten by a bird; the bird poops and disseminates more seeds; and then more yet more fruit grows (mediated).

In the first example you will be waiting for a return on your investment. In the second you won't. Because you could have thrown the seed into the garbage, but you choose to do it in fertile soil, now you can come back and collect the fruit. You did not have to take care of the plant; the external sources around it did it for you. But you did start the process.

Giving and receiving is a two-way flow. Oddly, only one way is promoted: giving. But what happens when you keep on giving and never receive? You drain yourself! You need to maintain a balance. Sometimes, you might even feel forced to receive something you do not want. It might be an object, a service, or even a communication. This will also weaken you, because you are being forced against your own desire.

This protective covering in your suit's design is going to prevent you from giving to the wrong person who might not be ready, or from giving so much of yourself that you cause yourself harm. It will also protect you from receiving what you don't want to receive.

Formula to prepare your suit's covering:

1. Give as much as you want give, but only if it *really* is your decision.
2. Accept only what you really want to accept. *You can always say no.*

Weapon: Wonder Woman's Lasso of Truth
When only protecting yourself is not enough, you need to fight back.

Falling into your opponent's provocations is letting him win. Look for the higher truth! The formula to craft a weapon like the Lasso of Truth is:

1. Be clear on the final goal: the goal must be to solve the situation, not to defeat the opponent. From the ethical point of view, what would be the best end-scenario?
2. Analyze the situation based on facts, not on ideas or prejudices.
3. Share the situation with those who can help you.

Now that you have your armor and your weapon, you can protect yourself from giving too much or receiving something you don't want; and have a way to focus on goals rather than opponents. But no superhero fights only with their brawn. Even Bruce Banner, The Hulk, uses his mind! So it's time to focus on improving what's in your head.

2. A processing and control center
We like to call ourselves rational beings. But, being honest, do you mostly base your decisions on cold hard facts, or on emotional judgments and ideas?

Cold hard facts will not always prove us right; sometimes, they'll show us that we were wrong. But they will give us more steady solutions that can be counted on and used.

Emotional judgments and ideas will probably make you feel like you win your fights, but they will also distract you from your greater goals.

To protect yourself from the second kind of kryptonite (stopping learning), you don't need a *new* gadget. You need to recognize – and correctly manage — the one you've always had, but haven't seen. I don't blame you. It's hard to see because it's not something that's in front of your eyes, but behind them: the brain.

Professor X's Cerebro

Cerebro is one of the most awesome superhero gadgets!

Professor Charles Xavier, one of the X-Men from Marvel comics, is an exceptionally powerful telepath who can read and control others' minds. He runs a private school to shelter and train mutants. In a world where mutants are seen as sub-human, Professor X's main goal is to create a peaceful world of coexistence and equality between humans and mutants.

His most powerful device is called *Cerebro*, which helps him find and help those with the mutant gene.

Now, think of Xavier's telepathy as your own ability to communicate without words, and to perceive the feelings, wants, and needs of others. To a certain extent, I'm sure you've done it. It's transmitting! Remember when we talked about that —how you influence people without ever knowing? As far as reading and controlling other minds, in a way, we've being developing that skill in this book. It is not that you are going to read a mind to know what that girl had for breakfast; it is that you will be able to predict her actions based on her behavior, and the knowledge that you are acquiring about heroes, villains, and everyone else.

A key point here! Mutants are a minority that stands out from the rest for being able to do what normal people cannot do. Most people see them as menaces. Professor X develops and uses his skills and gadgets to help mutants to be the best they can, and to promote a peaceful coexistence among everyone. Does that sound familiar to you, dear teacher?

How are you going to build your own Cerebro?

Cerebro means brain. There are basically two ways to build your brain: 1) as an organ, and 2) as your mind.

Although there is a lot to discuss about these terms, we are not going to go deeper into science, psychology, or philosophy. For our purposes, both the organ and the mind are intrinsically interconnected, and one influences the other directly. Therefore:
1. As an organ, you need to give it good rest, water, appropriate food, and exercise.
2. As a mind, you need to learn how to purge bad data and the beliefs based on

that bad data. It is also necessary to manage past experiences that slow your progress. At the same time, you'll be building your Cerebro with new and powerful information based on ethical facts that make sense to you.

3. A cornucopia

The irony of the middle-class is that most people, secretly or openly, wish to be rich; while, at the same time, making jokes and memes about money, and criticizing or even attacking the rich. In the book *Rich Dad Poor Dad*, Robert Kiyosaki says that one of the problems with the middle-class is that they buy luxuries before they can afford them. Why do they do that? It may be because it is an immediate reward based on emotions, and not on logical reasoning. This may also be based in the thought that "if I will never be rich, at the least I can experience that feeling for a moment".

There are plenty of books about becoming rich. This is not one of them. But in a material world, money is an essential resource that we need to know how to generate and manage. So, you need a cornucopia. Let's look at Iron Man's.

Tony Stark's unlimited creativity
What one man do, another can do. Do you remember this from Chapter 5?

Google "poor become rich examples" and see. What do those people have, or what have they done to achieve such a transformation? One thing is for sure: they are creators.

The same principle applies to any other resource. Think about having abundant friends, or time, or a spirit for adventure; you name it.

Tony Stark is a genius inventor –yes, also a billionaire industrialist playboy philanthropist— who uses his *technical* knowledge to create amazing mechanized suits of armor to help maintain peace around the world. He can do anything! From a suit that comes when you call it to a particle beam weapon; not to mention the self-contained life-support and environmental protection systems in his suit.

The keyword here is *technical*.

Technical:

1. Relating to the knowledge, machines, or methods used in science and industry.
2. Relating to practical skills and methods that are used in a particular activity.
    From Greek *tekhnē* "art, skill, craft"

Even rocket science can be learned. It is a matter of having a clear goal, finding the right information, aligning the right steps, and moving forward; keeping in mind that there is no magic pill, only a technical process.

How to apply this to obtain specific resources

To know it is *tekhnē*; it must contain specific parts and steps (a method) that you can learn and master.

Here are a few examples of the *tekhnē* involved in acquiring resources:

People: To choose mentors, coworkers, employees, and real friends, start with the 3 Zones Chart Guide. As stated in Chapter 4, there is science behind this.

Correct data: To look for what's been proven to work and follow those who have achieved success. Forget about mystery and good intentions.

Time: To control your action cycles (Chapter 11).

Money: The three basic keys on Chapter 12.

A couple more things about the brain
1. Neural connections

Understanding the way neurons create connections also helps you empower your brain and take control of what thoughts, experiences, or memories you wish to connect or disconnect. The more you pay attention to something, the stronger your connection to it is going to be. That is especially true when you not only think about it, but *act according to it*. It is like putting an extra layer of glue every time you send the same or similar information throughout your neurons.

> This can be good news or bad news depending on
> what you pay attention to.

There is an interesting video which explains this. I found it in YouTube with the name "Three Brains - Thinking to Doing to Being (Joe Dispenza)".

There you can see a short film showing the connections among neurons growing weaker or stronger according to the thoughts which are sent or received.

Think of all your neurons as having a limited amount of glue to spread around; that glue has to be distributed among the connections of every cell. So now let's say that you send three negative thoughts per one positive. More glue will be used to retain those negative thoughts. But if you start sending more positive thoughts, then more glue will be required for them, and so the neuron will have to take glue away from the negative connections.

Amazing! Isn't it?

Information + Emotion = Long Term Learning

The main neurotransmitters are triggered by emotions.

Emotions are the strongest glue in our brain. Information given to students without stories or without emotions will never form long-term connections for any of those students. It's not that they won't get it... it's that their *brains* will not have any glue to retain the information!

2. Brain cleaning service

Another awesome function of the brain is the way it cleans itself. While you sleep, the brain cleanses itself of both substances and thoughts that it does not need. This process is awesome! And *it's more important than you think.*

What gets washed away during sleep are waste proteins that are toxic to brain cells — it's one of the ways sleeping disorders can cause damage to the brain.

In terms of thoughts, the brain gets rid of those that it evaluates as unimportant. What's the criteria for the brain's removal? Those thoughts with less glue —the weaker thoughts— are the ones the brain removes.

Exercise 8.2: Clean and rewire your brain

An excellent way to build responsibility is by creating routines.
For this exercise, you will create a new routine for your sleep. It will include:

    a. Your sleeping hours.
    b. The thoughts you will print onto your brain before going to bed.
    c. The mood you will set, right when you wake up.

a. Write down the time you commit to go to sleep and to wake up. Make sure it fits your required amount (The average is 7-9 hrs. That can vary according from person to person. Make sure to check what's best for you).

Go to sleep _____ Wake up _____

b. For a few minutes, contemplate the image from Exercise 1, mentally adding every sensorial detail you can; that is: smell, touch, taste, **emotion**, noise, personal movement, and the like.

c. Wake up and smile! Think about three goals that you are sure to fulfill during that day and write them down. Stretch, dance, sing, or exercise for at least 5 minutes. Drink water.

How my gadgets worked for me

That frustrating and weakening experience from the start of this chapter, when I thought I had failed a school, pushed me to acquire gadgets that, at first, served as armor and a weapon to protect me; they now serve as tools to create.

I was being weakened, trying to help a group that didn't want to be helped. I didn't know that, back then. At the time, I made the mistake of believing someone who told me that I had studied too much already, that I had to do a reading (learning) fasting for a while, so I had stopped reading. Can you believe that?! I did! I was desperate. All my resources were very limited. Every step forward required a lot of effort, so a step backwards really hurt —it hurt emotionally, and it wasted resources.

Looking for answers, I broke my (stupid) reading diet. Based on what I learned, I used a different approach, built on a different foundation, and went in a different direction.

That happened about four years ago. Now I can tell you how much of a difference it has been. In short, in four years I've done four times more than what I struggled to do in the previous 20 years. Every time I do it again, it takes less time to create more positive results –because when you have the right gadgets, the kryptonite harms you less.

The biggest lesson I found in all of this, and from similar situations, is that an unsolved situation in one area of our lives affects every other part of our lives. In the example of the school, I was so focused on it that I gave less attention to schools that were doing a good job. It affected my physical and mental health, because I was worried I was not achieving my goal of helping those who needed it the most. This situation not only affected my profession, but it affected my health, my relationships, and even my pets and plants.

How could that be?

Let's talk about that in the next chapter.

CHAPTER 9:
YOUR 7 AREAS OF ACTION

The supervillain Satan, a legendary wrestler and powerful sorcerer, vowed to take revenge over the City of Guanajuato when he died.

As promised, 100 years after his death he came back and raised an army of mummies to kill everyone in town!

Jorge Pingüino, a known drunkard and tourist, tried to warn the city. Nobody listens... until it's almost too late.

Luckily, El Santo, Blue Demon, and Mil Máscaras —unstoppable wrestlers, fighting for good—were there on time to fight Satan and his mummies and save the city!

If you were born in the US, it is easy to relate to Captain America. If you happened to be Canadian, you might relate to Captain Canuck. For someone in India, I guess it would be Mr. India. But in Mexico, we relate to the superhero-wrestlers from the early 70s who fought mummies, aliens, vampires, zombies, werewolves, and even karate experts!

Different cultures have different cultural landmarks... so next time you hear "Think globally, act locally" don't think about changing *the* world, but *your* world. Although as human beings we share basic needs and wants, each of us has our own specific goals, our own specific wishes, and our own specific stories. Those who think they are "saving the world" –guilty as charged; I thought I was!- are actually changing themselves, and then joining tribes or groups who resonate with them. Those save-the-world individuals don't work alone. Everyone who wants to create their better world does so together, they help one another. While, somewhere else, whether we like it or not, there will be people joining together to cause destruction.

The world vs your world
Think of the world as a huge buffet, like a great meal served with all the kinds of food you can imagine.

Now imagine three different scenarios:

1. You take what you want and let others do the same.
2. You choose your food based on what is best for your health. You also suggest to others what you think is best for them too.
3. You are "sure" of what is best for you and others. You force others to choose certain foods, and do everything possible to get rid of what you think is bad.

What do you think will be the outcome of each scenario?

Of course, there can be many other options or combination of options for how these scenarios play out and start. But you get the point, don't you?

The world, then, will be the big scenario, the big game-board… and *your* world will be what you choose to do with it or in it. Pay attention! Here comes another vital formula:

The greater one's awareness,
the greater their capacity to create.

So there is the key: your capacity to create will be the difference between deciding what to do *with,* and *in,* the world. That is, between creating, changing, innovating *in* the world, and adapting the world to you, or adapting yourself to the world. This is the same as choosing to survive and transcend… or to succumb and disappear.

These words can mean a lot! But we can understand our life in this *world* better in terms of our Areas of Action as defined in Chapter 8:

1. Ourselves
2. Our significant other and our children
3. Our groups
4. The species to which we belong: humanity
5. The life that surrounds us: nature
6. The physical universe, including our belongings and environment
7. That invisible energy that we are: spirit

Earlier we talked about focusing on yourself first. That does not mean neglecting others. It is all about being aware that all change starts, *and ends*, with ourselves. That awareness can then expand to the other areas of action, and allow us to *act* on those areas to improve. That is why we call them Areas of *Action*, because there's movement implied.

Let's understand each of them separately so that you can manage them according to the results obtained in Exercise 8, part 1.

1. Yourself

Bliss, authority, respect, and success are built from oneself. They are not granted from the outside. *They are built from the inside.* The outside responds to the communications that we give ourselves; if our inside is tangled and upset, then the outside world will respond in the same way. If our inside is at peace and happy, then the outside world will respond in the same way over time. This is not easy. The outside world is influenced much more easily by confusion than by happiness. This is why it takes time.

It is easy to say... but hard to accept, because reality seems to give us different information.

It is possible that, among your students, you have seen more than one case of physical or mental abuse. There may be many cases in which familial or social environments are highly negative influences. In these realities it is almost impossible to think that their wellbeing depends on the individual (the student, in this case) and not on his relationships and his environment. I know; it was one of the most complicated mental debates I had for many years.

Just as you have observed those frustrating situations in which an individual seems trapped, surely you also know about those success stories where someone seemed to have everything against him or her then how, step by step, they completely transformed their lives and achieved the extraordinary! They are living proof that our well-being and growth depends on ourselves and our ability to internalize self-respect and the ideas of success. Without self-respect, and that initial idea of success, it is tremendously more difficult to ask the outside world for help.

We all have problems in our past that we need to exorcise. Some we can handle ourselves—but for most of them, we will need help! To deal with this in the best way possible, be aware and make use of these three pillars:

  A. Personal integrity and self-determinism
  B. A path to follow
  C. Allies and enemies

<u>A. Personal integrity and self-determinism</u>: In Exercise 7, part 1, you obtained an overview of yourself and *your perception* and the influence you have on everything that surrounds you.

In Exercise 7, part 2 you started working on *your self-determinism*. You started to shut up other voices to listen to your own.

In Exercise 7, part 3 you chose what to listen to and who you wanted to listen to, and by choosing only the strengths that resonate with you, you filtered through the opinions of others to keep only *what is real for you*.

In Exercise 7, part 4 is where you got to the thick of this!

Integrity: the quality of being whole and complete.

When you have integrity is, when you are whole, you are healthy, energetic, fit, abundant, fulfilled, and blissed!

B. Path to follow: if you don't know where you're going, any road will take you somewhere. But you already have a goal. You already worked on defining this a few chapters ago. Do you remember it? If not, go back to chapter 5, Exercise 5.1. Tape your goal to your mirror, so you don't forget where you are going. The more you lose sight of it, the more you are going to be distracted, and the longer it is going to take you to reach it.

Don't just write your goal down; write down the formula to make things happen (Chapter 5). This is the path to follow.

Allies and enemies: Now we are talking about people, based on chapter 4's breakdown of the good, the bad, and the confused.

The same way we cannot properly help anyone if we have not already internalized our Good, those who offer us help are not always be the best qualified to do so. Even if their intentions are good, they can cause more harm than good if they help us when they are not *ready to help*. It's important to choose correctly… remember what we said about not accepting help you do not want. If someone can help you, or you want them to help you, there are two things to make sure of: a) that they are in zone 1, the happiness zone, or as close to it as possible; and b) they have already achieved what you want to achieve; or at least that they have made more progress than you have, and know how to get from where you are now to where you want to go or that they can help you get to a point where you'll be more complete than you are now.

2. Creation: your significant other, children, and projects

We've talked about this. Everything we start doing, or continue doing, or stop doing, all affect *creation*—creation of happiness, relationships, art... those all affect how we *become* ourselves. I know, I said before that when we stop creating, we stop surviving and start to succumb. It is because we are used to thinking about creation as bringing something into existence, and that's very convenient! Let's keep it that way, but also stay aware that for something to be destroyed, there must be a cause that begins that destruction. Either something that was done, or something that stopped being done. A cause to an effect; therefore, a kind of creation. When you stop working out because it is tiring, you are *creating* a less-fulfilled version of yourself, even though you are destroying only one thing (your workout routine). When you begin reading history because you want to know about humanity, you are *creating* a better version of yourself—even though all you are doing is starting a habit (reading).

We basically *create* to experience and to transcend our lives. That's why this area of action is represented by our *significant other, children, projects and dreams*. These are all things that transcend our *own* lives and deeply — and completely — affect other people, and perhaps resonate far beyond our existence.

This is a key area, for it is the steppingstone to move into the other. Here is where we look for our soul mate, here is where we have our higher highs and our lower lows... but this is material for another book.

Do not dare to underestimate Creation! It is what every other area of action depends on.

> Every thought, action, inaction, and reaction is a step towards or against the creation of your highest and most powerful self.

3. Groups

Can you imagine your life without friends? Co-workers? Sport teams? Family meetings and social celebrations?

Of course not. That is the importance of this area of action. The way we contribute to the existence and success of the groups we belong to, directly impacts our moods, our energy, and our motivation. When you are aware of this, you stop thinking about your groups as something external where you just drop in and out as you please. *When you really understand this*, you take responsibility and do your best to contribute to the existence and success of each of them... and you choose better where to belong and where not to belong.

By uplifting the groups in which we spend our time (friends, workplaces, family) we are able to not just raise those around us into better zones of existence, but able to ensure that their confusion will not drag *us* down, and able to ensure that, when we have our own bad days or moments, when we *need help*, the people and groups we surround ourselves with will be strong enough to help us back up.

4. Humanity

What can I tell you that you don't already know about humans? You are a teacher. Why would you be teaching strangers if you did not believe in doing some good for humanity? You don't get to choose your students; you welcome anyone and do your best for each of them.

Looking around at newspapers, at news broadcasts, at the things we see on social media, I know that it can be very discouraging when we think about the future of the human race. Even so, our natural impulse to survive keeps us looking for that which works, and that which can keep us progressing as a species. And as little as it may be, it gives us hope and prompts us to act. As we act on all seven areas of action, we can raise up our groups and environments, and do good for everyone… yes, even humans we may never meet!

The world can seem discouraging at times, but there are people like you — millions, *billions!* — all around the globe, all trying to do the same thing… to become better versions of themselves, and to improve their own local communities. Always remember that, no matter how discouraging the news looks. Humanity is much more than what we see on TV.

5. Nature

Nature was here before us and will surely outlast us. In this area you will discover the ways you interact with other life forms, such as plants and animals.

It's amazing how those other ways of life relate to us to the degree that they can be indicators of our personal progress!

I remember a period of my life when even my plastic plants "dried up". Now that I've become more stable and am progressing steadily, any plant that I bring home stays pretty and healthy with even minor care… unless my cat decides otherwise.

Observe the way you relate to nature. Also note the phrases and the kind of language you tend to repeat. If you have posted something on the internet like "the more I know humans the more I love my dog" then there might be work to do in other areas of action.

(Love your dog. I'm sure it is wonderful. But also work to improve yourself, so that the humans around you improve by example, so that you can stop disliking other humans. Even the things we say in jest, sometimes, are things we secretly hold as true.)

6. Material

While we're talking about phrases like "the more I know humans, the more I love my dog" ...how about "Things look like their owners"?

That's weird. Why would an inanimate object look like the person who owns it?

Mostly unconsciously, we create and adjust our environments according to what we think we deserve, or according to the image we want to project. Personal integrity plays a very important role in this area of action. When you consciously decide what actions to take in this area, which includes your entire material universe, then you choose your belongings, and adjust your environments, according to what you like. Then you pick what is practical for you. You should choose according to what brings you closer to your goal, *not* to impress or please others.

Look at your surroundings. You might be able to learn something about yourself — and maybe it's time to change those surroundings. Remember! Every action has a reaction, right? That effect isn't *just* action... it's also presence. If your surroundings are ugly to you, or are doing your harm, it might be time to give your room a healthy make-over.

7. Spirit

Now we move onto the intangible and deeply experiential. Here we have that natural human impulse that moves us towards something deeper, something more relevant than simply living life. Some find their spirituality in religion. Some find it without ever touching religion. This is where science has a limit; how can a spirit be measured? How could its existence be proven with scientific methods? Even those people who claim there is no soul or spirit talk about seeing a spark or certain life in someone else's eyes or work. You can think of this area of action as being your muse... not just a creative muse, but a life-muse.

When we neglect this area of action, we become dull. Life seems to lose its brightness and begins to lose some of its meaning. That's why it's important to do something that feeds your "soul"—art, sports, cooking, *finding your tribe*... whatever! Make sure you do that one thing that makes you feel really alive!

Now, take another look at your drawing in exercise 7.1. What can you see now?

Let's see a couple of examples:

Think about someone who is devoted to helping her community; she spends all her time with her neighbors at church, or aiding groups in need, in order to be a good example for her children. But because she does all of this community work, she has no time to sit and help her children with their homework. How ethical is that?

How about a successful entrepreneur who smokes two packs of cigarettes a day and eats a lot of "fast food" and unhealthy food, and does work which sometimes harms other humans? A good amount of the money he makes will be wasted on those habits, and spent on current and future health issues. Because he has not been able to internalize his own good, and internalize self-respect, he allows himself to do these things to himself and to others and he doesn't even realize it.

Each of the seven areas of the Arithm-Ethic formula are closely interconnected. Neglecting one directly affects the others.

In the first example, this mother is sending the wrong message to her children. She wants to teach him the importance of serving others and connecting to humanity; maybe they are receiving that message, but they are also learning that helping others is so important that they should sacrifice their own family connections. That mother may have an A+ in contribution to humanity (fourth area), but how would you grade her at home and herself?

In the second example, the entrepreneur may have an A+ in the groups area (third area), but what about areas one, two and four? While the entrepreneur is making a lot of money, he doesn't take care of his own body — and the work that he does is making it more difficult for other people to be their best selves.

More on Personal Integrity

Your *brain*, your *spirit* and your *willingness* integrate together to form what you are within your personal space.

Learning barriers, antagonism and *lack of resources* are the main causes of the disintegration of your inner self; therefore, of every expression or creation that arises from it.

Your integrity is absolutely yours, and only you can keep it indivisible. Your interactions with the outside world can cause conflicts that divide and affect your integrity.

It mostly happens when we're dealing with people or situations that are pitted against our wants and beliefs; or with those who pretend to impose their ideas on us; or when we lose someone or something; or when we don't understand something and there seems not to be an answer or path to understanding.

The short answer to help keep yourself together and maintain your personal integrity is by being –and remaining– true to yourself.

Your brain is wired to recognize truth. You don't need to impose onto yourself somebody else's truth. Even if it sounds reasonable or like the "right" thing to do — if it is not true for you, it will not do any good for you.

Know that truth cannot be *imposed* on someone — on anyone. Truth is what it is, period. And the only way it will make sense to you is by observing and experiencing it by yourself.

Even this book! If you observe it, and experience it, and still it does not make sense to you, it will not be true for you. Remember: inner truth is always about something. It is based on facts or statements, but also on perceptions of those facts and statements, which many times will be different from person to person. If you find something in this book that seems logical to you, if similar experiences have happened to you, or you have come to similar conclusions or ideas, then it will be true for you!

> Personal integrity is what you know is true for you.
> It is to have the courage to defend your truth.
> Even if others do not agree with you.

CHAPTER 10:
REINTEGRATING YOUR INTEGRITY

"Anyone's capable of great good and great evil. Everyone, even the Firelord and the Fire Nation, have to be treated like they're worth giving a chance."

—Aang, Episode 3.16 "The Avatar and The Firelord"

I don't know if there is scientific research about this, but I heard somewhere that it requires the same amount of energy to pursue big dreams as it does to pursue small goals.

It makes sense if you consider that when you pursue small goals, it is because you are denying your amazing power to create! Fighting to constrain your creative potential sure requires a lot of energy!

I'm not going to sugarcoat it. I hope that you are reading this book not because you want me to tell you what you want to hear, but because you want the help to break through and to achieve your highest potential.

When you can't defend your truth and move towards your dreams, *when you give up*, you waste your energy creating excuses and justifying your inactions.

Unconsciously, you *create* obstacles to keep yourself away from your dreams. Sometimes those obstacles will hurt you without you even realizing they are there. This can be as mild as forgetting to set your alarm in the morning, or as dangerous as not being able to avoid an accident; and sometimes, it is a subtle thing, such as not taking care of yourself and becoming sick.

It is not rocket science! Observe your students and observe yourself honestly; we are our main obstacle to success! When we compromise our truth, we lose energy; when we defend it, we become stronger. Yes, the higher we rise, the tougher the obstacles. But as we move forward we learn to overcome them, and grow stronger still! You don't need to go far to find your own evidence for this: recall a time where you were at your best and creating constantly. Observe every detail. Smell it. Hear it. Taste it. Feel it. What was it like? Does it feel like you were sick? Like you were making mistakes? Were the obstacles making you frustrated and making you stop ? Or were they forcing you to rise up and overcome them? At that time, you were naturally doing well.

On the other hand, recall a time when you were sick, had an accident, or were making unusual mistakes. What, or who, were you avoiding? What were you afraid of? What were you doing that was against your beliefs and your truths? Maybe you were being too cautious to avoid disappointing someone. You were trying to do "good" – or, to do what *others* define as good.

Remember, we are defining good and bad from an ethical point of view: that which benefits the most Areas of Action and damages the least, is good. That which damages more Areas of Action, and benefits the least, is bad.

Are we inherently good or evil?

There were endless debates in my philosophy class discussing whether man was naturally good or evil. About four centuries after Hobbes and Rousseau's opposite theories of human nature and morality, scientists are now more inclined to believe we are basically good. But, if so, how do we explain all the evil around us?

An article by Adrian Ward in *Scientific American*[6] lists a set of studies, carried out by diverse groups of researchers from Harvard and Yale, and discusses whether our first instinct when dealing with others is to act selfishly or cooperatively.

Those studies were framed by a dual process of decision-making in terms of two mechanisms: intuition and reflection. Ward defines these studies' understanding of intuition as "often automatic and effortless, leading to actions that occur without insight into the reasons behind them."[1], and reflection as "conscious thought—identifying possible behaviors, weighing the costs and benefits of likely outcomes, and rationally deciding on a course of action."

Intuition was identified with selfishness, and rational reflection with cooperation. Their opening question was *"Do we cooperate when we overcome our intuitive selfishness with rational self-control, or do we act selfishly when we override our intuitive cooperative impulses with rational self-interest?"*

---

[6] https://www.scientificamerican.com/article/scientists-probe-human-nature-and-discover-we-are-good-after-all/

The final results favored altruism. There was evidence that, in their words, "it seems that we are an overwhelmingly cooperative species, willing to give for the good of the group even when it comes at our own personal expense", and that "we seem to be hard-wired for altruism".

To me, this sounds like they are saying that it is selfish to consider your own welfare before the welfare of others. It is good to think of others, the conclusion says, but bad to think of yourself. The article even ends by saying "…it seems that we are an overwhelmingly cooperative species, willing to give for the good of the group even when it comes at our own personal expense."

Is that really a good thing?

First me, or the others?

You already know the answer. We went through it in the seven Areas of Action in chapter 7.

In a way, there's not much separation. We separate them the same way we separate subjects at school: to have a better understanding of the whole by understanding its parts.

At school you teach your students subjects such as grammar, logic, biology, math, physics, morals, and ethics. But in real life everything happens at once: Mike goes to the store, communicates with the clerk, looks for something to eat, decides what's better for his body, picks something according to his budget, makes sure not to put the eggs under the watermelon, pays, says thank you, and smiles.

Mike is thinking of himself first, while also taking others into account. He is polite, respects the store's environment, and if someone needs help, he could be ready to offer it. Misunderstood altruism will tell you to *sacrifice* yourself for the good of others. That is not altruism; that is martyrdom. Altruism, from Latin *alteri*, dative of alter "other", does refer to others, but does not necessarily require forgetting about yourself. From an ethical point of view, it would be you taking care of your 2nd, 3rd, and 4th areas of action (creation, groups, and humanity).

When *first me* becomes evil

To understand this better, let's separate people into two groups according to their social behavior.

Table 6, Cooperative vs Non-Cooperative

Group 1: COOPERATIVE	Group 2: NON-COOPERATIVE
These people are closer to the heroes than to the villains; therefore, they tend to be confident, helpful, aware of the present, and look with hope to the future.	These people are closer to the villains than to the heroes; therefore, they tend to be afraid, problematic, stuck in the past, and have no hope for the future.
MAIN CHARACTERISTICS 1. Recognize real harm. 2. Is specific (Mary said that, this watch is expensive…). 3. Enjoys sharing good news and looks for the good side of a story. 4. May alter a communication to delete injurious matters, trying not to hurt people's feelings. 5. Avoids causing trouble. 6. Solves problems as per their capacity. 7. Finishe what they started as much as possible. 8. Takes responsibility. 9. <u>Provides real help.</u> 10. Supports others to succeed. 11. Responds well to treatment or help.	MAIN CHARACTERISTICS 1. Haunted by imaginary enemies. 2. Generalizes (everybody says, everything is expensive…) 3. Focuses mostly on bad news, or the bad side of a story. 4. Alters communication. The more drama, the better. 5. Causes trouble. 6. Poor problem-solving. 7. Hardly finishes what they start. If finished, their work will have careless mistakes. 8. Blames others (they avoid responsibility). 9. <u>Is destructive while claiming to help.</u> 10. Hinders the success of others. 11. Does not respond to treatment or help, even though they may pretend they do.

Now, that you are aware of this, ask yourself: who is good and who is evil? Who, according to Characteristic 9, is altruistic?

The non-cooperative

> Santosh Patel: You think tiger is your friend. He is an animal, not a playmate.
> Pi Patel: Animals have souls. I have seen it in their eyes.
> Santosh Patel: When you look into his eyes, you are seeing your own emotions reflected back at you.
>
> Scene in The life of Pi (2012)

In that scene, Pi, a young good boy, was trying to feed, with his bare hands, a huge Bengal tiger. His dad showed up just in time to save him!

It is very hard for good people to see evil intentions. Not only that, but when evil intentions become evil actions, good people still believe that deep inside there is a good lost soul that only needs some love and help – I know this first-hand. In a way they are right! ... But while that good soul is hidden or kept captive by confusion or aberrations, we had better learn to recognize and manage the danger of the villains.

Villains are people with great amounts of confusion. Unlike good people, they think everybody is a wolf in sheep's clothing. They see themselves as the good ones, and the others as enemies. The same way the tiger was seeing prey in Pi while Pi was seeing a friend in the tiger.

Going back to what we know about villains, it is their dark pasts that trap them and keep them from moving up toward fulfillment.

Think of *Crime and Punishment*, written by Fyodor Dostoyevsky in 1866. It gives us a wonderful view of how a man deep in the confusion zone, in the name of help and altruism, destroys his Areas of Action.

In Dostoyevsky's story, Raskolnikov, the 23 year old protagonist, is poor but has strict moral codes. His goal, based on his beliefs and application of his moral codes, is to finish his law degree so he can help poor people as a lawyer — which was, he thought, his mission on earth.

Raskolnikov met a rich and despicable old woman – a pawnbroker. He viewed her as evil because of her job as a pawnbroker; then thought that killing her and stealing her money would remedy that evil, while improving his own life and improving the life of the poor around him. He kills her and then kills her step-sister. He does not succeed in taking much of her wealth, as he was too disturbed by his own acts.

There were no witnesses. It was the perfect crime. There was no way anyone could figure out that he was the murderer.

As the story continues, you can see how Raskolnikov's primary intention to help becomes problematic in each of his Areas of Action. He goes through a tempestuous love relationship with Sonya (area 2); his friend becomes his accomplice (area 3), and Raskolnikov ends up getting rid of the stolen goods, confessing the murder, and being sent to a Siberian prison (area 1). Not only did he not become a lawyer doing good in the world, but he did not help his family, he damaged every relationship he had and, of course, thought he lacked anything of worth to offer humanity (area 4).

He could have got away with it. But he didn't! Why?

A couple of answers

1. We are inherently good. Our very basic impulses are altruistic, because they are aimed at our survival, which depends on each and every one of our Areas of Action—including those which involve other people. We may hate our neighbor, but, if her house is on fire, we will not hesitate to help. That "being hardwired for altruism" helps us survive as a species.

Those who are not filled with regret and problematic pasts, or those who have been able to control their regrets, are able to think more rationally and achieve more effective results; thus, achieving progress in each of their Areas of Action. These people are in The Cooperative Group.

Those who are excessively burdened by their pasts may have their decisions influenced by impulses and emotions, and may cause more harm than help. These are in group 2: The Non-Cooperative.

2. As a consequence of that inherent goodness, when we commit a harmful act, we expect punishment. This applies to people in both groups. What makes it different for each individual is their ability to assess the situation, and their capacity to solve it.

Those in the lower levels of confusion won't be able to handle the situation, so one of these two things will happen:

- a) They will continue to cause harm until punished or controlled.
- b) They will hurt themselves. It might be as mild as withdrawing from others, or as intense as not taking care of themselves — not sleeping, not eating — and suffering from an illness or an accident.

Of course, this occurs mostly without conscious thought. But the moment you become aware of it, you can take responsibility, control your impulses, and move forward.

Think about our Raskolnikov from *Crime and Punishment*. He becomes ill immediately after the crime, and lies in his room semi-conscious for several days. He gets mad every time someone tries to help him.

Now it should be easier to understand why there is no perfect crime. Even if there are no witnesses and no way to find out who committed a crime, most criminals will leave traces and clues behind... or punish themselves.

How to favor the cooperative

By controlling the non-cooperative, period.

But... how do you do *that*?

Controlling the non-cooperative

Have you ever trained a dog?

Once I gave myself the challenge to prove my educational theories on a troubled and somewhat dangerous deaf English bull terrier. What a challenge!

I adopted him when he was 4-5 years old. Because of his deafness, he had not received any kind of education or training. As he grew up, before I adopted him, he became more active and, because he had not received any education or kindness, dangerous; so he ended up chained in a back yard, and remained that way for years! Finally, Bruce, as I named him, was rescued by an animal protection group, which is how I got him... after he'd had four previous homes, where he had been given to other people and then returned because "he was a lost cause."

After 4 bites –one of them immobilized my right hand for one month– countless broken ornaments, and plenty of destroyed furniture, Bruce became the most adorable and happy dog he could be.

What did I have that the others didn't? Authority and control.

We learnt about authority already (chapter 6), and we'll talk about control in the next chapter.

Authority: Bruce's past and instinct led him to be dominant and defensive; he reacted to all new experiences according to his bad past experiences. I had a new plan for him! I was the author of a new future for him. I had to become an *authority* for the dog, and firmly lead the way. How? Making sure that my plan included what was important for a dog. I gave Bruce enough room to feel free in a place with clear and strict boundaries that would make him feel protected and under control and, at the same time, led him towards the final goal: a well-trained, happy dog.

Freedom: the right to live the way you want without being controlled by anyone else.

Do you know exactly what it is that you want?

How many people do you know, who know exactly what it is that they want?

There lies the problem with uncontrolled freedom. Absolute freedom cannot exist in social groups. There are norms and set boundaries that exist so we can interact with other people.

That was one of the very best lessons I learn from Maria Montessori[7]: we should not grant children freedom until they have learned to follow the rules.

A child in a Montessori environment can freely choose a material to work with, but is not "free" to take a material from another child or destroy a material, or leave a project incomplete on the table and to go to start another one. He has to finish the cycle and bring the material back to its place. This is freedom with controlled boundaries that allow the child to learn by experiencing freedom in a well-planned and controlled environment that will lead him to developing a habit of seeking conclusions and finishing action cycles.

What I constantly observed in Montessori's "classes" was a very calm, happy, cooperative, and creative environment. When I replicated it in summer camps, the same thing happened. Non-cooperative children were very rare, because they were in a controlled area where they could feel safe. When problematic situations did occur, they were easy to handle.

Now I've been observing the same phenomena in regular classrooms; when disruptive children are controlled, the rest naturally become more cooperative among them. They

---

[7] Montessori, M. (2013). Freedom in the school environment, didactic material and teacher.

even show empathy to the disruptive child who, in many cases, gradually gains self-control and self-discipline, and joins the cooperative group.

What happens is that when the environment is consistent, structured, and predictable, the people within it are at peace. Knowing what to expect reduces stress levels and makes people happier with responsibility. When someone knows what to expect, and is able to manage it, they slowly rise up from the confusion zone and towards the good zone.

Bonus: a great way to control a non-cooperative person is by giving him very specific tasks –avoid Q&A. The clearer and more specific, the better: a clear beginning and end, numbered steps, and some room for creativity in the process. Give them no more than 5 steps; 3 to 5 is best. If the task requires more steps, split it into smaller tasks. It is important to make sure they have a clear understanding of what is expected of them. Acknowledge when they finish the task, and encourage their own search for solutions when a difficult situation arises or when a mistake is made.

CHAPTER 11:
TIME MANAGEMENT

Control is not only about solving situations with people and environments; it is about having time.

A day lasts the same amount of time for an idler as it does for a leader of a nation. How come the first cannot change his own life while the second can change the lives of millions?

Lack of time is the first complaint I always hear from teachers; yet, the most successful teachers I've met never say "I don't have time!" They say something like "Sure! Let me check my calendar." They may have a little room in a week, but they know it because they have an organized calendar. They know what they are doing, when they'll do it, and how. They start and finish what they plan. The easiest way to recognize them is by their perfectly organized classrooms.

"Do not worry about being organized. The mess sends a message to others that we are such busy people that we do not waste time being pretty." -A former boss.

Hearing my boss say so was very convenient for me. I was a teenager at the time; not having to worry about being organized allowed me to focus on more interesting and fun stuff. After all, it was my first job, and it was at a dive shop. Lots to learn and enjoy!

He found it funny to see me putting together a regulator after maintenance, because I usually ended up lacking the pieces to complete it, or had some left over. As you may guess, the fun didn't last long. As a consequence of the lack of organization (control), the service we provided to customers was poor. The complaints were so frequent that they were normal; they became something we expected. We justified ourselves by saying: "tourists are rude! No one will ever satisfy them."

39 years later, that dive shop is still recognized for its bad service and its number of complaints, which include some life-threatening accidents.

The most amazing thing is that neither my former boss, nor his successors, could ever see the relationship between control and efficiency. Every failure was always someone else's fault. It was never the fault of poor or non-existent organization.

Control is the key to efficiency

Efficiency: "power to accomplish something," from Latin *efficere*, to effect; to be the cause of a positive effect.

Efficiency is to *really* do what you say you'll do; not to act *like* you're doing it.

Somewhere in the world, there is a person who turns on his TV –not sure what to watch– has lunch, then does the dishes; on the way to brush his teeth, he notices that the dog needs water, and fills up the dog's dish. The smell reminds him that the dog needs a shower and nail clipping; so he goes to the bedroom for the clipper. Once there, he forgets why he's there. He takes off his sweater and throws it onto a pile of clothes which accumulates over days, then he goes back to the dining room and get trapped by an irresistible offer on TV. Who doesn't need a cup which warms itself?

What just happened here? He finished 3 out of 9 activities that he started: 1) had lunch, 2) did the dishes, and 3) filled the water dish. Six tasks were started… and may never be finished. 1) the TV is still on, 2) his teeth are not clean, 3) his dog is not washed, 4) his dog's nails are long, 5) his clothes are messy, and 6) he's thinking about (but probably will not) buy a magic cup.

Formula #4: Measure efficiency

$$Efficiency = \frac{tasks}{results}$$

Efficiency is measured by the obtained results, not by the time invested in getting them. Those who don't understand this are the same people who cannot understand why a professional will charge more than a friend of a friend. Don't fall for the "I'm very busy" and "I don't have time" excuses. Someone efficient will always find the time and the way to do what really interests him; also will know when to say no.

According to the formula, our example person has been 30% efficient. He thinks that it is ok; he forgot to brush his teeth, so what? He'll be fine. And for the rest, it all can wait; it's not the end of the world!

What he doesn't know is that unfinished tasks keep on consuming energy, in units of attention, until finished or released. It is like opening programs and apps that you are not using; they are still consuming RAM memory. He is taking with him every unfinished task, project, or idea that has been started and not continued, or continued but not finished. It includes maybe buying the magic cup, or thoughts of the business he may one day start; it includes the call he is afraid to make or receive; the health issue that hasn't been resolved; the wall that needs painting; the bunch of unused objects that are accumulating over the years; and the promised coffee with a dear friend. And, of course, his smelly dog.

Control is predictable change. It is the ability or power to decide or strongly influence the way in which something will happen, or someone will behave.

Control is the ability to handle <u>complete</u> action cycles.

Action is the key word! Control is not a negative thing. It is the difference between making things happen and things happening to us.

It is quite common to think of control as something negative and/or imposed. That is because it is used as a synonym of *stop*. What's the first thing that would come to your mind if one of your students was misbehaving, and the principal happened to stop by your class and said: "control that child!"

The first thing thought will be to *stop* that child!

But to stop is only the last part of the anatomy of control: **1. Start, 2. Continue, 3. Stop.** Those three parts are, of course, the steps of a complete action cycle. Those are also the three characteristics of motion. So, every action of yours is, by itself, an action cycle. Therefore, every action *requires control*. And yes, being aware of our own scopes and limitations helps us to control ourselves from hindering or dominating others – which is not the kind of control we are talking about.

Steps of an action cycle
1. Start
You are in the woods and want to start a campfire. So, you get everything ready, light a match and make sure the fire gets to the tinder, twigs, and branches.

The cycle does not start with the idea. It starts with actual action, when you start giving life to an idea. Think about the idea as the seed of the action. If it is a tomato seed, it may not take much room in your kitchen while waiting to be planted. But if it is a coconut... you'd better do something about it.

While an idea is in your mind, it is using units of attention, and making you feel bad because you know there is something you want or have to do, but that you are not doing. In the very moment you decide and put action to the idea – that is when you start taking control of it.

2. Continue
Now that your campfire is nicely burning, you want to keep it going by adding branches; and want to keep it safe by not letting the fire spread beyond your fire-pit.

In this step, you keep on provoking and maintaining the change without deviating from your final objective. You have started to act on an idea; it must now be continued.

3. Stop
Ok, you already roasted marshmallows, performed your favorite songs around the camp, and had fun. It's time to put out the fire. Here is when you make sure you extinguish it completely.

When you stop, you make sure that the objective is fully accomplished. You make sure you are not leaving any loose ends.

It is that simple... right?

Well, if it was, everyone would reach their goals. Something as "simple" as writing an email can be overwhelming for many: "How do I start? Oh, this is too cliché! Do I go right to the point or be nice and follow social protocols? Now, Gosh! I can't stop! What should be the right final words?"

Why is it so hard?!
Compulsive starters
There are people who find it easier to start... and start, and start, and start, and leave a bunch of tasks started. They may seem very motivated and enthusiastic, but they just start and leave it all there; the action is either abandoned, or someone else has to take responsibility for it. This kind of person's attention is everywhere!

Compulsive continuers
There are those who can continue a task but can't stop. They are usually afraid of doing something wrong. Here is the student writing the perfect essay; the artist giving endless

"final touches" to his piece; or the teacher accumulating tons of materials for a project that keeps on extending instead of delimitating towards a clear and specific goal.

Here's also the person that goes from job to job, friend to friend, and project to project. He is constantly changing the goal, and therefore will not follow instructions correctly, and never will achieve completion.

A compulsive continuer has very little control over his life and environment.

Here is where my former boss was! Leaving open cycles gave him a sense of importance because "he had too much to do". But the truth is that *he wasn't doing much*. He was only doing the same thing over and over, and making the same mistakes over and over again.

Compulsive stoppers
These are the most dangerous of the three. That is because they have very little control of themselves and their environment, so they reflect that into others by stopping them. Here you find the one that prevents you from changing, creating, or innovating because it is all a "lost cause", or "it's too risky", or it's bad, or dangerous, or whatever they have to say that will make you stop.

The worst are the hidden ones. Those that seem to be nice or funny, the ones that would say something like "I know you are busy, but…" It's that awful "but" that makes you stop, predicting an unwanted yet unavoidable deviation. "Are you wearing a dress or a piñata? Haha, I'm kidding, you look fine" — would you go happy to the party after that? Probably not! In some way, they have stopped you. "I know you want that so bad, that's why I'm telling you that it's a bad idea, because I don't want you to be disappointed" – even if you don't stop, you at least have second thoughts.

We, who are responsible for education, must be especially careful not to stop compulsively. We have learned it for generations, which is why it is so difficult to realize how often we do it. Do these phrases sound familiar to you? "Don't run! You are going to fall!"; "Wait! You don't know how to do that!"; "…you are going to get sick"; "…you can't".

Compulsive stoppers are the ones who make us think that control is a bad thing.

How to make it easier

Remember that unfulfilled dreams and ideas, as well as unfinished tasks, *keep on consuming energy*. They trap units of attention until finished or released.

The less control you have over your action cycles, the less motivated or energetic you will be.

The next exercise will help you experience the fabulous feeling of recharging and gaining motivation as you become aware and take control of your actions.

Controlling the self
Exercise 11: Controlling personal action cycles

For this exercise, recognize your incomplete cycles as every action that you have had in your mind as an idea but haven't started, or that you started but did not continue, or that you continued, but never stopped.

Know that an action cycle can be as short as feeding your cat, or as time-consuming as creating a successful business. Action cycles can go from making a phone call or finally saying "I love you"; to changing your look, or your living room; to fixing your motorcycle, or developing new income streams.

Instructions
1. In column 1, make a list of every incomplete cycle that you have in each of your seven Areas of Action (Chapter 8).
2. Decide if you are still interested in each, and if you *really* are going to put the needed resources to finish it. According to it, write Yes or No in column 2.
3. For every "No", decide whether you are going to forget about it, throw it away, sell it, give it to somebody else, or whatever! Just get rid of it.
4. Assign priorities to the "Yes" in column 3. Use 1st, 2nd, 3rd..., or High, Medium, Low.
5. Following the formula to make things happen, *make it happen!*
6. Celebrate or give yourself a reward every time you complete a cycle.

1 Incomplete action	2 Still interested?	3 Priority

Tips

1. Handle one cycle at a time.
2. Visualize or write every step of the cycle (start, continue, stop) in as much detail as possible.
3. Divide the most difficult tasks into small goals.
4. Ask for help. You don't have to do it alone.
5. Assign times and dates; create deadlines.
6. Use the "do not interrupt" sign –be aware of the compulsive stoppers.
7. Focus on the task you are doing. Keep yourself in the present.
8. Push yourself to do your very best without overwhelming yourself.
9. Make adjustments as you move forward. Your goals are yours and yours only; you can always change your mind, just make sure to complete the cycle.
10. Congratulate yourself!

Controlling others

As a teacher, you do not have a choice. You have to control your students.

But now we've agreed that control is a good thing! Think about it like a board game. There, everyone must follow the rules and control their own cycles. No one can keep the dice forever, ready or not. They must be thrown! Pieces must be moved — even if this will make you lose! And you can't play it forever; no matter how much fun you are having, it must, at some point, stop.

So, that's how you control others:

1. **Make sure everyone knows what's going to be done, and to what purpose.**
   That is, make sure everyone knows the game that is going to be played. Purpose is key! Most of the time it is going to be you who picks the activity that your students will do, and they may follow it like robots because that is the way they've learned. But if they find a why and their own motivation to do the activities, then they'll get something more out of it. This can be done by making them agree with you. One way is to ask very simple questions that stimulate their interest in the subject.

2. **Establish comprehensive and attainable rules.**
   Exactly like a board game: very few, clear, and unbreakable rules that everyone can remember and follow. A good rule of thumb: have three to five rules that you count with your fingers, and have the students repeat it using their own fingers.

3. **Help them to control themselves.**
   They have to recognize their own action cycles and manage them. Be careful to only guide them to see or do what they cannot see and do by themselves.
   This may be the hardest part for you, because here is where you have to control yourself and avoid compulsive acts. The moment you play the game for them, everybody loses.

4. **Let them make mistakes.**
   Mistakes are how we all learn… so when your students make mistakes, let them force themselves to find solutions so they can take their capacities to the limit. Next time, they will be able to go further. Keep an eye on them, and give them enough room to try different ways to solve a problem. The only time you get deeply involved is when the situation starts getting beyond your students' capacity to control the action cycle. In those cases, let them know that it is part of the process, and that there is nothing wrong with not always having the answer.

5. **Teach them to be aware of the larger cycle and the smaller cycles within it.**
   If they are going to plant a tree, the finished larger cycle will be a planted tree. The smaller cycles will be the steps that'll get you there. So, make a list of micro cycles, and make sure to recognize the fulfillment of each of them:

   a. Dig the planting hole. "Good!"
   b. Place the tree in the center of the hole. "Yes! Right there!"
   c. Build a soil berm. "There you go!"
   d. Water the tree thoroughly. "Great! You're done!"

Lists work like a charm! Create them, teach students how to use them, and help them follow every step to the end.

A couple more things to consider:
1. Shifting from a tyrannical mode to a mode of healthy control will take some time. But once your students learn to control themselves, everyone will achieve more in less time. All of you will experience the real meaning of efficiency and fulfilment.

2. Keep in mind that you will be controlling different kinds of players. Some will be afraid, most of them confused and, if you are lucky, there may be a hero or two. For that, remember that you already have the tools to control arising situations. You have **STAnd** and the Zone Action Guide Table in Chapter 4.

I bet you will be amazed at how you will have more time as you acquire control of your action cycles.

CHAPTER 12:
MONEY

My cousin´s bedroom was magical! I just needed to open his closet and I could become Daisy Duck or a wrestler in minutes! We played as much as we wanted with all these costumes, toys, and games, and ended afternoons in a warm and bubbly bathtub. A weekend with him and his parents was like a movie where I got to experience what it was to go to a golf club, and to go shopping and choose what made me look pretty – without having to worry about the price. It seemed natural for them! So, I thought having money should be natural.

I was only 7. I could only be aware of was in front of me: these people seemed more relaxed, their surroundings were prettier and in better shape, they didn't have to do it all because there were people in charge of the different tasks, and guess what? I never heard them talking about money! They were not complaining about it, or criticizing the rich, or making bad jokes about money or about people who had money. Therefore, what I thought that having that kind of life was a matter of attitude.

Those "movie weekends" didn't have a happy ending. Going back to my own family's reality, I was punished or ridiculed for behaving like "a rich girl", as my siblings and my granny called me when I did something that reminded them of my cousin or his parents. So I learned to fit in both worlds... while being totally confused for years.

During my spiritual pursuit, money didn't get any easier to think about. You know, money and spirituality seem to be opposing forces, and I, in a way, thought so too. But it made more sense to me to think that even as spiritual beings, we exist in a material world where we have agreed to use money to exchange goods between us –that doesn't make us less spiritual.

More than 40 years later, I've come to see that my cousin's family life was not as perfect as I had thought when I was 7, but for sure had better opportunities because they had more money, and were more able to manage different exchange mediums. It's not just money-in, money-out! Sometimes a lot of other mediums and exchanges are involved, which makes things complicated... but I learned this. If we do not have the goods we'd like to have, it is partly because we don't know how to manage different exchange mediums, including the use of money to trade for goods.

The end of my second life in this lifetime
"Wow, mom! It's like you had lived two lives in this life."

I can't recall exactly *why* he said this, but it was something Leonardo, my youngest son, told me when he was 14 after watching me delivering a paper in a Philosophy Symposium.

I had never thought about it before—and Leonardo saying it really made me stop and think on it. It became the beginning of my journey to improve education and help less fortunate children. My previous life as a scuba- and free-diver could not have been more different... especially the money side of it.

I've told you before about my life as a diver, but now let's view the financial side of it.

Scuba-diving is a very profitable industry. I got my first certification at the age of 14, and started my own diving business when I was 21. I had no administrative knowledge or experience managing a business, and no initial investment fund. Despite that, the business grew up fast and I made some good money. I enjoyed diving so much that I didn't care about being rich. I cared about going out to the spots I liked the most and about having the most advanced and nice equipment that allowed me to feel good and which got the best performance both in and out of the water. I cared about learning, training, sharing... seizing every moment. At the same time, I was interested in the Montessori school my kids were attending; I attended every educational seminar and conference I could, no matter how much they cost or what part of the country they were in.

"Magically", during that time, I didn't struggle for money. It is not that I had that much money to spare, but I always had what I wanted. I was as focused on what I enjoyed the most as I was focused on my goals, and I never doubted I'd reach them.

After 20 years as a diver, I did have to learn how to live a different life. I moved to my *second life,* with the goal of getting more knowledge to guide my children, and also to go beyond and fuse education and my scuba-diving background. Being a former below-average student –all the way to high school– I had never imagined that I would become such a nerd! And I was happy when I decided to become one. I had never imagined that I could spend the rest of my life studying, teaching, researching, and delivering papers.

First, I planned to continue the diving business. But there were many elements there that made it impossible. So I took two jobs; one as an English teacher in a private school, and the other as content director in an online academic journal's index. Neither of them paid very well. But helped me during my time as student.

Those were very hard years. I gained knowledge and discovered abilities that I never thought I had, and I'm still very grateful for everything that contributed to my foundation, including key elements of my Magic Wand. But it came with a big price: I had almost no family life (I was out from 6:30AM to 9:15PM); no time to dive, go to the gym, or exercise at all; no way to eat healthily; and no money.

In contrast to my *first life*, in the second, money was scarce. All those philosophical and spiritual guilty concerns about material goods were not very helpful. My master's degree, even though it was in administration, didn't change that pattern much, because it was about administrating non-profit institutions, like schools. Truth be told, now I know that schools can be very profitable! But back then, my surroundings and beliefs didn't allow me to see that.

During that time, I was barely able to pay for my studies, could take no more trips, and had no time for hobbies; I sold all my diving stuff –including my fancy, cutting-edge personal equipment and gadgets— and my debts increased.

What had just happened?!
I stopped enjoying life, and my Areas of Action got out of balance. It became more about doing what I *thought* was right (moral behavior) than about doing what *was right*. I started that career to create my dreamed diving university, and, somehow, I ended up delivering a non-profit program to public schools. There's nothing wrong with that. But that was not my dream… and that shortage of money continued *for 12 years!*

What happened then?
With the precious help of my mentor, I became aware of what had happened. I realized how and why I made mistakes that diverted me of my dream. It was exactly when I learned the Aritm-Ethics that I shared with you in chapter 7.

It was August, 2017. How could I forget? I was so shocked! It was like watching a movie of my life from an objective point of view. More than a movie, along that month, I went through various chapters of my past that enlightened my present. My present felt like falling apart because the structure holding it was made of moral beliefs, not ethical principles. It was so fragile that I had to be making a great deal of effort to keep it together. Do you remember the part we talked about using as much or more energy to to stop us than to move forward? Well, this is a perfect example.

But, guess what?

As soon as I was willing to firmly defend my integrity, and not to compromise my truth, I recovered my superpowers and started to build a new life. Farewell my second life, welcome to the third!

Believe it or not, my income almost doubled in a very few months! That was outstanding, considering that I had been making about the same amount for 12 years. Now, writing this book two years later, my life is totally different. I have new dreams, new plans and, finally, I can tell that my life-long pursuit of answers that I can trust will work is paying off.

Transcend Your Money Limitations

As a teacher, you may not be interested in becoming a rich and successful entrepreneur, but I bet you agree that being financially free and stable will allow your creativity and life to flourish.

Remember what we said back in Chapter 8. "There are plenty of books about becoming rich. This is not one of them. But in a material world, money is an essential resource that we need to know how to generate and manage." We talked about a cornucopia then, about how to generate and manage money. What follows are a few lessons I've learned about money, and how to manage and generate it to become financially free. It is mostly about removing, or at least making less obstructive, tight or painful finances.

This is what I've found to be the essence of my experiences, several books I've read, and trainings I've received about money.

To start, here are three basic keys:

1. Make a list of all of the information to make extra money that you can find.
2. Pick the ones that work! Those from authors that walk the talk. From those, go with the ones that make sense for you.
3. Apply the **STA**nd formula (Chapter 1).

In number **1**, dedicate all the time that you want. Sooner or later, you will start finding similarities among them all. There is where you will naturally move to number **2**. Number **3** is Aladdin's magic lamp: Stop to clearly recognize your possibilities and your resources (foundation/start). Think in the most objectively and ethically way possible about your whys, whos, and hows (steps/continue); and take Action (goal/stop).

What I've learned from those three keys is:

A. Money is an agreement, not an object.

The main and only reason that money exists is so that we can value goods and services and exchange those goods and services with greater ease.

An agreement is a negotiated and binding arrangement between parties with different points of view. Therefore, there will be different agreements between lower-class, middle-class, and upper-class people. Totally different points of view! I think that the famous phrase "You are the average of the 5 people you spend the most time with" has something to do with this; but I would extend this to your groups. Here is where you need to be careful of who you listen to, and who you agree with. Keep in sight the Cooperative and Non-Cooperative chart from Chapter 10.2.

B. Money is the medium of exchange

by which human beings have agreed to live whether or not they know it.

Exchange is an act of giving one thing and receiving another. It can be as little as a smile, or as massive as a piece of a country. The trick here is to learn and master the art of exchange. There are many types of exchanges, but the following is a pretty good example of one you might be familiar with.

If you stay up until 3:00AM preparing a great class, and the next day your students don't care at all, would you do it again? Or, what if you don't prepare the class at all, and all your students, who are eager to learn, are let down by your lack of preparation? Will you be able to gain their trust again?

Once you learn which kinds of exchanges to give and accept, and which to avoid, you will gain control over those exchanges, and have an easier time predicting the outcomes (remember Control from Chapter 11).

Kinds of exchanges to accept

      a. Abundant: You give more than it is expected, and happily accept when

others give you more than expected. The best "more" is in value, like interest, follow up, or a good attitude.
   b. Equal You give what it is expected, and receive what is expected; no more not less.

Kinds of exchange to avoid
   a. Unequal: You give less of what it is expected from you. You receive less, of what it is expected from others.
   b. Criminal: You give nothing in exchange for something, and receive nothing in return. Others give you in exchange for something, and you give nothing back.

These kinds of exchange may seem convenient for the side that kept more and gave less but, in the long run, affects their personal integrity and reduces their chances of success (remember chapter 10).

C. If you work for money, that's what you are going to get (that's not good news).

That's all you are going to get!

Do you want money? Or what you want is what can be bought with money?

There are tens, if not hundreds, of stories of unhappy rich people. It is not money that solves your problems and achieves your dreams. It is you who decide the path of your life and, when necessary, decide to use money to move through it. Some paths need more money than others; it's up to you to decide when you need which path.

On the other hand, there are blissful rich people out there. To start, notice that I'm not saying happy, but blissful, which makes us think of a deeper and long-lasting contentment; this results from deeper, more meaningful, and long-lasting goals. That's what these people have in common.

That is, if your goal is to live and look like a celebrity, once you are there, it's done! Now what? But if you go for a greater and long-lasting good, it may or may not include living and looking like a celebrity, but your journey won't end there. Because on the way, there will always be more to do or a better or different way to do it. **This is important for you to know, and to keep in mind!** Because not knowing it has caused me many, *very* frustrating moments: when you go for deeper and more meaningful goals, **life becomes more meaningful.** You set a big and almost unreachable final goal to use it the same way sailors use the North Star: to keep you from getting lost. They'll never get there, yet it keeps them moving; and every experience along the way is an experience worth living.

Now, what is a deeper, more meaningful, and longer-lasting goal? The one you found by dreaming big and thinking ethically. That is, the one that considers the greatest good for the most of your areas of action. It can be the one you envisioned in Exercise 0, at the end of the introduction, and the one in Exercise 5, in Chapter 5.

D. If you focus on your main goal,
then money will be a medium to get it – one among many.

Fellow introverts, this is especially for you.

The exchange we're talking about is always between people. We need to interact and connect with people to know what services or goods we can provide that they see as valuable... so that we can get something from them that we think is valuable.

As an exercise from an entrepreneurial program, I, as part of a team, had to start a business that earned $100 in 90 minutes... and we started with only a match! The challenge was greater for me considering that the rest of my team were even more introverted than I was! That program meant a lot to me, so I had no choice: I had a **non-negotiable goal**. What would have you done?

85 minutes left; a single match; no plan; and four scared teammates. I had no time for my predispositions, nor time to fear failure; all I was able to see was my goal. I didn't have all the answers and I would not waste precious time trying to find them, so I just took step one: offered the match in exchange of whatever somebody would give.

Barter was effective at the dawn of humanity. To barter, you need to talk to people and find out what's valuable for them. What are they willing to give you in exchange for something that you have?

First I got a pen for the match, which I traded for a thread bracelet, then for a sandwich... and it continued until it became a thermos which, with the help of my team who were getting excitingly involved, we decided to raffle. At the end of the 90 minutes, we made $74. But the lesson was so valuable!
As soon as I stopped hesitating and focused on my goal, the channels for money to flow

showed up.

Think again on your answers in exercises 0 and 5. Are they still the same now that we have come this far? If you want to make adjustments, go ahead! Then, see how both goals are connected. Now start focusing on them, and on the many resources and mediums that can get you there.

5. Based on the previous points,
you must create channels for money to flow.

Money is not simply an amount of production alone; it is also the quality you must deliver to ensure exchange.

Working on my own **STA**nd formula, on the **T**hink step, I observed the superior data (see chapter 5, *Let's do it the right way*, point 2) from most of the books and trainings I've had about money and finances. From my top favorites –*The Science of Getting Rich* by Wallace D. Wattles (1910), *Rich Dad Poor Dad* by Robert Kiyosaki (1997) and Grand Cardone's Playbook (2016)— I got this formula that I now share with you.

Formula #5: Create Money Flows

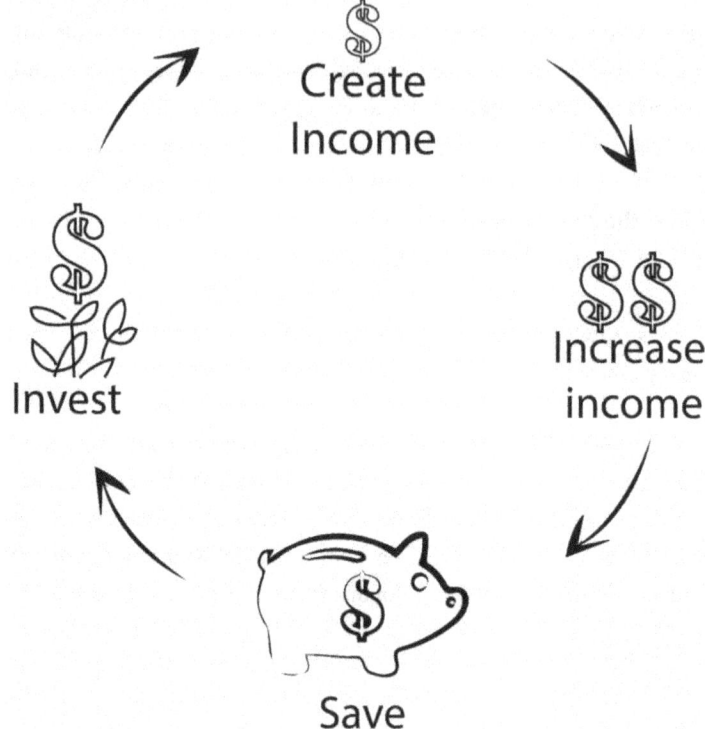

Step 1. Create income

It is very likely that you already have a job. In that case, all you have to do is keep it and move to Step 2.

If you don't have a job, get one! It doesn't have to be the job of your dreams. It just has to give you enough money so you don't starve, and so you can work on the rest of the steps in the formula.

Step 2. Increase income

This is not about getting a new job. It is about keeping the one you have and doing something in the same field to help others while helping yourself.

"Are you crazy?" "No time!" "I already have two jobs!"
"I need to relax, not to work more!"

That's what I hear when we get to this step. That probably happens because:

a) You haven't worked on the Control Formula.
b) You think you are working because you have to, not because you want to.

If a) is your case, commit to identify your action cycles, and to finish them. Make it a habit! Start gradually, committing to find and control one cycle a day; then two, then as many as you can handle. Knowing that you can decide when to start, continue and stop will help you leverage your time, and give you peace of mind.

About b)… well, that needs a special approach that cannot be worked on in this book. For now, it will help you to know that that the present job that you may not like is your step 1. Without it, you cannot take this step 2. You may leave it in the future, or end up loving it –it happens quite often. For now, it is your steady base.

Good news: we are living in an era with lots of opportunities to work with our minds, not with our hands. Machines are doing the hard and dirty work for us. This is the time to make your hobby give you a financial return. To do what you like most, what you are good at; and to share it in a way that you can generate some additional income from it.

In this step, you will think about ways to increase your income in your field. It is not time yet to go from teacher to astronaut. A good idea is to freelance your talents in places like Guru, iWriter, or 99designs.

Embody your new Superhero Style (Exercises 2.1 and 2.2; Chapter 2); and Act! Here is where you build your authority (Chapter 6).

Don't think right now about large sums of money; focus on value exchange. This is the way to open channels to increase income.

The following exercise will help you understand and apply this step.

It's fun time!

Exercise 12.1
Do some Google searches about business ideas from home. You'll find hundreds. Somewhere, you will find one that matches your abilities, capacity, and interest.

A) Which of those fit your interests, knowledge and skills, and can be of value for people around you? Write them down.

Brainstorm
-
-
-
-
-
-
-
-
-

B) Think of different ways that you could trade each of them, either for money or any other resource.
-
-
-
-
-
-
-
-
-

C) Explore among your acquaintances and use Google for information about someone who is doing something similar, and how. What's working for them? Can any of them mentor you?

-
-

-
-
-
-
-
-

D) Using the previous example of turning a match into money, and following the Formula to Make Things Happen, go ahead! Make a plan to **increase your income!**

1. Write your ethical and clear goal

2. Detail your logical steps to connect the goal with the foundation

3. What constitutes your foundation?

Step 3. Save

Until now, you have not spent a nickel unnecessarily! And you still won't. Not yet. As Grant Cardone says, "Pay the price now, so you can pay *any* price later."

That doesn't mean that it has to be boring or painful! It means that you are changing your mindset. Now, you do not celebrate your success buying beers; you do it... I don't know... by doing nothing at all, maybe; or dancing naked on the grass; or spending one full day of leisure without feeling guilty. Don't spend money on celebrations yet! And if you must, make sure that the money you spend is a small amount. You don't want to set yourself back with a large purchase or party.

In Step 3, you'll keep on using your income from Step 1 for your daily expenses, and save your full income from Step 2. Remember that you didn't have it before, and you were coping without it. Ok, hold on a little more! If you spend the money from your new source, you will never move to Step 4.

Step 4. Invest

It is time to go further.

This step is about reinforcing the good results of exercise 12.1. Look back on everything you've achieved until now. Acknowledge your successes and think of ways to reinforce them. Now you have the money to do it! Maybe you will pay a good mentor, buy cheap objects to sell them for more, or enroll in a workshop to learn profitable skills. Just make sure not to waste your money on promises. No speculations, no "coaches" that will not give you real steps sustained on real, proven numbers. Keep your investments as small or large as you can — always make sure that you have full control of them.

In this step, be very careful to keep your levels of progress well-balanced (Exercise 7.1). And *do not listen to naysayers*.

It's fun time! Again!

Exercise 12.2

A) How can you improve what you have been doing to increase your income? Think in terms of the Pareto principle, which states that roughly 80% of results come from 20% of the causes; for example, 80% of sales come from 20% of clients. Find your 20%, and write what you can do to reinforce that 20%.

-
-
-
-
-
-
-
-

B) Who is doing something similar to what you're doing, **and succeeding?** What's working for them? Can any of them mentor* you?
*Check Chapter 6 again.

-
-

-
-
-
-
-

C) Make a plan according to the Formula to Make Things Happen, and **increase your income!**

1. Ethical and clear goal

2. Logical steps to connect the goal with the foundation

3. Solid foundation

Step 5. Repeat

The income from your present job, plus your new revenue flow, is now your Step 1. Make sure to maintain it, so you can start the cycle again, only with larger figures. If becoming better in your present job won't improve your income... Stop, Think, and Act.

The number one mistake people make once they have a stronger source of income is to spend it. Wrong!

When Step 4 is giving you money, this is what you do:

1. Economize: Now, money should be steadily flowing. The first, and worst!, mistake people make here is start spending. This money should be used to:
    a. Pay every bill.
    b. Invest the remainder in service facilities for your proyect and make it more possible to deliver.
2. Discover what caused the best flows of income, and strengthen it.

Remember: create, increase, save, and invest.

What's next? repeat the formula.

When do you stop repeating the formula? When you get out of the Rat Race, as defined by Kiyosaki and *Rich Dad Poor Dad*:

> The pattern of get up, go to work, pay bills; get up, go to work, pay bills. People's lives are forever controlled by two emotions: fear and greed. Offer them more money and they continue the cycle by increasing their spending. This is what I call the Rat Race.

Ascending spiral

A rat races in the same wheel the same way over and over again. That's *not* what you want to do!

You are going to repeat the Money Formula in an ascending fashion, and gradually create flows of income that will not depend on your full-time presence. As a teacher, no matter how good you are, you can only teach so many hours a day; but if, for instance, you create a special video training, and sell it, then that video could be making money for you even while you're asleep!

PART III
THE GOAL

CHAPTER 13:
NOW WHAT?

...Well, this is why we call it *lifestyle*.

It is to live a life with style. A style consciously chosen by you. *That's* what's now.

The Cambridge dictionary defines style as "a special quality that makes a person or thing seem different and attractive", while the Wiktionary defines it also as a "characteristic mode of expression, particularly one regarded as high quality".

The style you created in Chapter 2 is an expression of your inner strength which will make you seem different and powerful. There is nothing more attractive than someone who is authentic; someone who doesn't need an artificial style borrowed from a magazine or anywhere else.

When you create your own lifestyle with a meaning, that is, one based on your own self, and aimed at a goal that is worth striving for, there won't be a "now what?" moment. As soon as you achieve one goal –even as you're *approaching* completion! you'll already begin thinking about the next.

And that's a life that is worth living!
Make creating goals and going after your dreams a lifestyle!
Your Superhero Lifestyle.

Remember that when you created your superhero lifestyle in Chapter 2, you defined your secret identity (like Diana Prince, Clark Kent, or Bruce Wayne). Now, after all we've been through together throughout this book, you know the real secret: your secret identity is really just you! This is you, being you, and enjoying it! Have fun with it!

Innovate or *die*

It looked like when a parade had finished. The place was a mess! There was trash on the floor, chairs and tables out of place, people leaving in clustered crowds, and some rushing back for things they'd left behind.

It was a high school classroom, for God's sake! That was fundamental education! And worst of all... the teachers didn't seem to care!

I was the new teacher in that classroom. I went to the principal to find solutions, or propose some... only to find that she didn't care either. She asked me to be patient, and not to ask too much from my students; that this school was their only option. These students were not accepted into any other school; some for their lack of learning skills, most for bad behavior –which made it *almost* impossible to develop learning skills. She asked me to do my best to help them move on, finish, and get their high school certificates. That's all their parents were worried about; parents who, by the way, "could be not bothered" with complaints about their children.

Instead of being patient, as the principal asked, I used my Magic Wand. Instead of doing my best only to help them get their certificates (as the principal said), I helped them develop basic skills to move forward by themselves, in school *and* in life. I know for sure that it was life changing for some, because of what they shared with me later. I stayed in that school for just one quarter. *It was not my style.*

In a way, I innovated; but within very narrow limits. Three 45-minute classes a week per group didn't give much room for steady growth. With the time, continuing would have meant me swimming against the current forever. Salmon swim against the current, but not their whole life. They do it to spawn, and then they die. They spend most of their lives in the ocean... and as a diver, I'd had to deal with currents many times. You *deal with them*, don't swim against them. You find a way to not have to swim against the current by holding a rope, flowing with it, parallel or perpendicular, just long enough to find still bodies of water.

I used to think that it was my duty to try to fix everything I saw wrong... because if all humans did that, we would finally live happily ever after. But you know what? No matter how convinced we are that something is wrong, it is happening because someone else thinks it is right!

In that school, everybody accepted this: keep the teenagers busy long enough to give them a certificate and let them go. They were convinced that was the right path. For me, in that school, handing out a certificate to "let a student go" is giving them a lie that will affect them and their future employers. Because one day, they will have to prove that they have knowledge and skills that they don't have. But for every reason I gave in defense of my point, the rest of the school community had three reasons to say I was wrong.

Every environment is created with certain goals, beliefs, and agreements –whether they're good or bad is out of discussion for now. We build our personal environment and can only help contribute to other people's environments. Therefore, if we don't like a certain environment, and if most of the people think it is okay, or agree it's wrong but are not willing to change it, then *we're* the one that has to change! That's the kind of innovation I'm talking about here.

Innovation: a new idea or method, or the use of new ideas and methods.

Innovating ourselves with new ideas or methods is the best way to manage such situations and environments.

In our own environment, we set every single detail the way we want to see it, and the way we want it to be used. If somebody enters our environment, we'll do as much as needed to maintain the way that things are. It's true for a countries, cities, towns... and schools. If I'm the one visiting a new environment, I may see things that can be improved; but my decision to improve them or not will depend on a number of factors.

There are places or environments from which you don't leave easily, or from which you aren't supposed to leave. When that's the case, you have to pay closer attention to how to choose your Magic Wand... and very importantly, pay close attention to which mentors can better help you use your Magic Wand to achieve a goal, a dream, or to protect yourself.

Sadly, most people choose to adapt to difficult environments, as it's the easiest thing to do... but it's also the easiest way to a slow death. *Innovate or die.*

As dramatic as it may sound... it's true. Most people choose to adapt, so the less you follow that current, the fewer people you will find thinking like you are –we already talked about this. There will be fewer people, but those people will be full of life! Those are the teachers who teach, even when they're in different professions.

Please, don't get confused; not swimming against the current doesn't mean you have to follow it. I said deal with it, manage it; look for calm waters! Calm and clear waters. Those which are clear because they are alive and constantly regenerating. Not calm, muddy, and stinky waters.

Let it go

To make creating goals and going after your dreams a lifestyle, you need to learn to let go. To teach by example, you need to learn to let go. To innovate, you need to learn to let go.

Think about it. What happens when parents don't let their children go? Or when teachers condition their students in such a way that the students only flourish under the leadership of that one teacher?

A few days ago, I was telling a friend how I was gradually moving to work remotely with my coworkers. He asked me if I was not afraid of them taking the company in their own hands, to make it their own if I wasn't around in person. "Afraid?" I thought. That's exactly what I want them to do! **That would be the final proof of a work well done! A system built to do good.** Where everyone involved is there because wants to be there, making it their own, and doing it well!

In order for our programs to transcend, I had to document every successful procedure, as well as every possible situation, and ways to handle all these. That way, those after me would benefit from my knowledge and experience; it was all in written. That's the way you let go of techniques, methods, and teachings; you pass them down. But how do you let people go? **By guiding them correctly, and letting them think and experience by themselves.**

> In *The Last Jedi,* when Luke was planning to destroy the Jedi texts, Yoda appeared and burned down the tree himself. This was a collection of ancient texts which contained the first teachings of the Jedi Order! Someone had written all those texts to pass down all of that important knowledge. Luke had learned the rules –based on the experiences of those before him. It was time to continue on his own. "Look past a pile of old books," said Yoda.

You see? To let go means to create and to let your creation create a life of its own. It means to give, *really give,* without conditions. Aren't you the happiest when a student of yours finally gets it, and proudly celebrates her or his achievements? We all like recognition, but if as soon as she or he starts celebrating then you take the credit, you are not letting them go. In that moment, you undermine their self-esteem, and your third area of action (remember, that's your groups) goes down, weakening the rest. Our recognition comes later, and it can come in many shapes and many ways, not necessarily when, how, or from whom you think it should come. What other profession moves someone to remember you, and smile, say your name with a "thank you, wherever you are" four, five or more decades later? Have you done that? Have you remembered the name of professionals of your past?

Let me guess, you remembered the name of dentist of your childhood, right? Of course not!

But you do remember your teacher's name, don't you? (Sorry dear dentists).

Recognition: from Latin verb *recognoscere* 'know again, recall to mind'. It is to learn again.[8] How do you want others to learn from you again in the future? To recognize you?

How would you like to be re-cognized?

Better yet: how do you re-cognize yourself?

Think about the past—we've gained so much from it! How ungrateful would we be to not recognize it! *Historia, magistra vitae!* Yes, what a teacher history is! And the best way to be thankful to a teacher is by learning lessons and applying them in our present, and applying them to improve our present life.

Despite how much the old times are missed, or how much they hurt!, they are *old*. They are the past. To innovate, you have to let them go. Enjoy the good memories and learn the lessons! ...And let them go. Because that's what you do when you make creating goals and going after your dreams a lifestyle: you complete cycles, and move forward... which takes us to the last part of what prevents people from finding goals, and the last part of the "now what" moment after achieving a goal: incomplete action cycles.

Never-ending continuum
Believe it or not, one reason why some people do not close action cycles is because they are afraid they won't have anything else to do once the cycle is complete. They continue and continue and continue, all to avoid reaching that "now what?" moment.

---

[8] https://www.lexico.com/en/definition/recognize

When your goal is higher than what you consider possible, but still you go for it, you will be reaching "smaller" –and still very rewarding— goals that will prompt you to the next goal and next action cycle. You will be acting in complete cycles, each of them taking you to higher goals, therefore to higher levels of control. You will not get to the "now what?" because you will know in advance what's next.

It is very easy to get trapped in routines and to lose sight of a goal. That's especially true when the process is giving good results, and opens new paths that you follow by inertia. The same is true when it is going wrong. When things go wrong, we become trapped because as we fix one problem, two arise. Hence, the importance of managing action cycles. If you don't close a cycle consciously, it will be stored in your subconscious, along with units of attention; as we discussed in Chapter 11. Things will start going wrong to a point that you will have no choice but to **Stop**. From here you can **Think**, **Act**, and start over. (Remember: always ST**A**nd.)

Pay attention to the red flags.

Exercise 13.1: Main Red Flags Check List

1. Vague goal and/or no bigger goal to pursue after the current one.
What is the exact expected outcome of what you are doing?
_____
Is the outcome worthwhile?
_____
What do you want that outcome for? Does it add to a bigger goal?
_____

2. Lack of purpose.
Why are you doing what you are doing right now?
_____
Why are you a teacher?
_____
Is that *why* aligned with *your* real needs and wants?
_____

3. Fear.
Are you excessively planning and/or correcting to "deliver perfection"?
_____
Are you afraid of not getting what you thought you would get?

Now What?

What if you got a different outcome? What's the worst that can happen?

What would you do if that different outcome happens?

Stop

Now what? Stop. That's it.

Stop: *transitive verb*; to finish doing something or end it, or to cause someone or something to finish.

You have the right to just stop. Somehow, there is this belief that teachers should be active all the time... and teachers end up not only believing that, but believing it's *right!* But it is healthy to stop once in a while, you know? That's the good thing about avoiding never-ending continuums: you consciously stop. Then, you decide what to start, and when to start. Now you can do that because you have a clear point A, a clear point B, and can consciously, and at will, decide the best way to connect them. How does it feel to have that power?

Exercise 13.2: Completions

a. From column 1 in Exercise 11 (Chapter 11), pick the actions that you marked as "Still interested" in column 2.
b. Add them to column 1 in the table below.
c. Fill columns 2 and 3 as per their titles.

1 **Action from Exercise 11**	2 **Was it completed?**	3 **If yes:** Write your achievements. **If no:** What are you going to do about it?

CHAPTER 14:
START – CONTINUE – STOP – **REPEAT**

"Wax on, right hand. Wax off, left hand. Wax on, wax off. Breathe... in through the nose, out through the mouth. Wax on, wax off. Don't forget to breathe. Very important. Wax on, wax off. Wax on, wax off."

Mr. Miyagi, The Karate Kid (1984)

The mind accepts something new by reasoning, learns it by repeating, and achieves with discipline.

<u>Reason</u> (n) from Latin *rationem* (nominative *ratio*) reckoning, understanding, motive, cause, from *ratus*, past participle of *reri* "to reckon, think. Intellectual faculty that adopts actions to ends; also "statement in an argument, statement of explanation or justification.

Do you have now enough reasons to believe that a Superhero Lifestyle can change your life, and *the lives of your students* for the better? If you do, congratulations! You are ready for Repeat.

How many times should you repeat the formulas?
Well, tell me how many times Usain Bold had to repeat his training routines to achieve eleven world and eight Olympic titles as a sprinter. Tell me how many times your mom helped you to tie your shoes.
It will depend on your goals, your desires, your decisions, and how far you want to go.

It will be **discipline** what will keep you going. I've found this to be the hardest challenge for most people: be disciplined enough to keep on repeating until you achieve the final goal.

> "Think about it as training a hamster to go through a labyrinth. Every time you find him climbing out, peacefully, firmly grab him and bring him back. If he's going in the wrong direction, he'll find out and look for a different path. If going too fast, too slow, or doesn't feel like going; give him time... or incentives now and then."
>
> –A Buddhist monk.

Funny thing, by the time that monk said that to me, my son was training a lab rat at home. The lesson could not be clearer! Have you ever tried hitting a little rodent to teach him something? ...well, don't do it if you want to keep him alive.

Train your inner hamster at your own pace. Start-Continue-Stop-*Repeat*. Every repetition will take you up on an ascendant spiral that can take you as far as you dare to go.

To help you with *Repeat*, here is the book in a nutshell:

To keep in mind
It all started when I realized that the main problem is not the undervalued teaching profession. The problem is that

the main purpose and intention of the educational system is to teach lessons about succeeding at **school**, not about **succeeding at life**. And **so many teachers** have been taught to think **about school-success and not life-success.**

Doing what's "right" is not going to make you happy. Enhancing your skills, freedom, and creativity will.

Rules of the game: Do the best you can, with what you have, right where you are.

Somebody is watching you!
Our students deserve, *and need,* teachers that show their inner power with the satisfaction and pride that comes from a well-used gift. They deserve it as much as you deserve, *and need,* to know that you are highly valuable and indispensable – despite what others could have told you.

Teach by example
The best teachers are those who had already accomplished what they teach. They learned it by studying, experiencing, making mistakes, and finally, succeeding.

Ethics are rationalized morals

Ethics obeys what is essential for the greatest good. It goes beyond specific beliefs, local needs, or limited timeframes. Once you start making your decisions based on what is ethical, and not only what is moral, your life will improve dramatically!

Save yourself first

You're not going to be able to help others if you don't protect yourself first.

Not only the good ones have superpowers. Do not underestimate the villains.

Be the author of your own life

Be the **author**ity in your space... then expand your space.

You are not alone. Find your Yoda, better yet, your Yodas.

Gather or create your gadgets, and protect yourself from kryptonite... better yet: **defeat it!**

It helps a lot to understand our life in terms of our seven Areas of Action:

1. Ourselves
2. Our significant other and our children
3. Our groups
4. The species to which we belong: humanity
5. The life that surrounds us: nature
6. The physical universe, including our belongings and environment
7. That invisible energy that we are: spirit

Make creating goals and going after your dreams a lifestyle!

A Superhero Lifestyle!

Reachable and *realistic* goals will take you nowhere.

The outcome from your goal should make all the effort worthwhile.

There's no way to know it all in advance.
Yes, make a plan, but focus on making it happen, not making it perfect. You can fix anything on the way.

It won't be all rosy
...but will be worthwhile!

The Formulas

Formula #1: STOP, THINK, and ACT

STOP, and observe and recognize the general environment. Stop impulses to react without control. Stop moving, and break the inertia of beliefs, customs, and practices that refuse to let you think. Open yourself to new ideas, and to new points of view. Stop and take a moment, so you can Think.

THINK what your steps are going to be. Think on your whys, your hows and –highly important— your whos. Focus your attention completely on your goals, on what you see as being the purpose of it all! Do not think about what you wish to avoid. Focus on moving forward. Think carefully, but not lengthily; because you have to Act.

ACT, even if you are not perfectly prepared –you will never be. There is no way to foresee everything that can happen. Begin to act, aware that at some point you are going to fail. And when that happens, rejoice! Because you will find the out point; you'll be ready to improve. **This is the way to make things happen!** The only thing you must not do is fail in the same exact way. Learn and keep on going.

Formula #2: Make Things Happen

1. Set an ethical and clear goal

    The more detailed and clear your plan is, the more likely it is to happen. The more ethical it is, the more satisfactory your results will be.

2. Build a solid foundation

    You are the foundation of your own life and everything that happens in it! It is a constant formation throughout your life. Invest in yourself as much as possible, even if you look forward and cannot see the end. If you keep on building yourself, sooner or later you will look back and see your achievements, enjoy your gains, and feel safely supported by a steady base.

3. Connect 1 and 2 with logical steps
   Don't try to eat the elephant in one bite. Cut it into little pieces and eat it one bite at a time.

Formula #3: Arithm-Etics

The level of **Ethics** is directly proportional to the level of **progress you achieve**, starting with **yourself, and then** the groups and surroundings in which you exist, while you maintain your own **personal integrity**.

This is all about you. It is you who build your own **you** —**with integrity!** - so that you can grow and succeed. It is never about others. You interact with others and are influenced by them, or they're influenced by you, but, in the end, it's always on **you** to improve yourself.

Simple arithmetic: adding, subtracting, multiplying, and dividing:

1. The level of ethics is directly proportional to the level of progress (*add* levels as you reinforce yourself).
2. The progress starts with the individual (*subtract* the individual from the group, and focus on the individual).
3. The progress then expands to a wider range: to the collective (*multiply* the benefits).
4. The individual maintains his personal integrity (*divide*… and rule!).

Formula #4: Measure efficiency

$$Efficiency = \frac{tasks}{results}$$

Efficiency is measured by the obtained results, not by the time invested in getting them. You become efficient when you are able to control.

> To control is the ability to **start, continue,** and **stop** an action. That is, to complete action cycles.

Formula #5: Create Money Flows

Step 1. Create income: Get a job.
Step 2. Increase income: Keep your job, and open a new flow of money.
Step 3. Save all the money from your new flow.
Step 4. Invest your savings to increase your extra flow.
Step 5. Repeat on a higher scale.

More than words

What started as a guide to share principles and formulas to make your life as a teacher easier ended up being an autobiographical book. Quite astonishing, coming from someone who barely shared about herself for most of her life. Yet, here it is, me, teaching by example; jumping again to a new adventure.

For every tool that I have shared with you, there are many more out there; I'm sure you have some good ones! For every formula, there may be specific requirements for special situations or needs. For every piece of my life that I've opened up to you, well, there is material for books in every genre; everything from tragedy to comedy, and why not? Science fiction!

> My granny's noodle soup was the most delicious soup I have ever tried! Luckily, she taught my aunt and my mom, and my mom taught me to do it. Sadly, although we all have the same recipe, and use the same ingredients, none of them taste the same. Even though we still make and eat good noodle soup.

Here's my noodle soup for you. It is what has kept my body, my mind, and my soul healthy. But that's not the best thing about the soup! The very best is to see how it warms up the whole being after the first sip! It is when others taste it, when I see others experience it that I really, fully, enjoy it!

Then, it is when I think "If only we all did this, we would all be happy/successful /there would be no poverty/hunger/injustice...". But, we've gone through it. Either we'd like to accept or not, we live in a perfectly balanced dual universe where there is day and night... as well as good and bad. Which is why there cannot be an "If only we all did this". So, maybe it is not about saving the world, or about legacy, but about mental health; or about liberating ourselves and discovering new ways, or better yet, new universes.

Don't be what the world needs;
choose what you want to be in the world.

A last piece of advice: Hang out with people who fit your future, not your history.

BONUS

24 Qualities That Geniuses Have In Common

The world's greatest geniuses have all had 24 personality characteristics in common, and you can develop the same traits in yourself, says an expert.

"Most people have the mistaken idea that geniuses are born, not made," declared clinical psychologist Dr. Alfred Barrios, founder and director of the Self-Programmed Control Center of Los Angeles and author of the book, TOWARDS GREATER FREEDOM AND HAPPINESS.

"But if you look at the lives of the world's greatest geniuses –like Edison, Socrates, DaVinci, Shakespeare, Einstein –you discover they all had 24 personality characteristics in common.

"These are traits that anyone can develop. It makes no difference how old you are, how much education you have, or what you have accomplished to date. Adopting these personality characteristics enables you to operate on a genius level."

Here are the 24 characteristics Dr. Barrios lists which enable geniuses to come up with and develop new and fruitful ideas:

1. DRIVE
Geniuses have a strong desire to work hard and long. They're willing to give all they've got to a project. Develop your drive by focusing on your future success, and keep going.

2. COURAGE
It takes courage to do things others consider impossible. Stop worrying what people will think if you are different.

3. DEVOTION TO GOALS
Geniuses know what they want and go after it. Get control of your life and schedule. Have something specific to accomplish each day.

4. KNOWLEDGE
Geniuses continually accumulate information. Never go to sleep at night without having learned at least one new thing that day. Read. And question people who know.

5. HONESTY
Geniuses are frank, forthright and honest. Take the responsibility for things that go wrong. Be willing to admit, "I goofed", and learn from your mistakes.

6. OPTIMISM
Geniuses never doubt they will succeed. Deliberately focus your mind on something good coming up.

7. ABILITY TO JUDGE
Try to understand the facts of a situation before you judge. Evaluate things on an open-minded, unprejudiced basis and be willing to change your mind.

8. ENTHUSIASM
Geniuses are so excited about what they are doing that it encourages others to cooperate with them. Really believe that things will turn out well. Don't hold back.

9. WILLINGNESS TO TAKE CHANCES
Overcome your fear of failure. You won't be afraid to take chances once you realize you can learn from your mistakes.

10. DYNAMIC ENERGY
Don't sit on your butt waiting for something good to happen. Be determined to make it happen.

11. ENTERPRISE
Geniuses are opportunity seekers. Be willing to take on jobs others won't touch. Never be afraid to try the unknown.

12. PERSUASION
Geniuses know how to motivate people to help them get ahead. You'll find it easy to be persuasive if you believe in what you're doing.

13. OUTGOINGNESS
I've found geniuses able to make friends easily and be easy on their friends. Be a "booster", not someone who puts others down. That attitude will win you many valuable friends.

14. ABILITY TO COMMUNICATE
Geniuses are able to effectively get their ideas across to others. Take every opportunity to explain your ideas to others.

15. PATIENCE
Be patient with others most of the time, but always be impatient with yourself. Expect far more of yourself than of others.

16. PERCEPTION
Geniuses have their mental radar working full time. Think more of others' needs and wants than you do of your own.

17. PERFECTIONISM
Geniuses cannot tolerate mediocrity, particularly in themselves. Never be easily satisfied with yourself. Always strive to do better.

18. SENSE OF HUMOR
Be willing to laugh at your own expense. Don't take offense when the joke is on you.

19. VERSATILITY
The more things you learn to accomplish, the more confidence you will develop. Don't shy away from new endeavors.

20. ADAPTABILITY
Being flexible enables you to adapt to changing circumstances readily. Resist doing things the same old way. Be willing to consider new options.

21. CURIOSITY
An inquisitive, curious mind will help you seek out new information. Don't be afraid to admit you don't know it all. Always ask questions about things you don't understand.

22. INDIVIDUALISM
Do things the way you think they should be done, without fearing somebody's disapproval.

23. IDEALISM
Keep your feet on the ground –but have your head in the clouds. Strive to achieve great things, not just for yourself, but for the betterment of mankind.

24. IMAGINATION

Geniuses know how to think in new combinations, and see things from a different perspective than anyone else. Unclutter your mental environment to develop this type of imagination. Give yourself time each day to daydream, to fantasize, to drift into a dreamy inner life the way you did as a child.

-L. Ron Hubbard

"If we have our own why in life, we shall get along with almost any how."
Friedrich Nietzsche, *Twilight of the Idols*, "Maxims and Arrows."

ABOUT THE AUTHOR

Lucía Briseño Haro, with a rare mix of scientific, spiritual, administrative, and philosophical thinking, has been a pioneer in diverse and successful endeavors which, as years have passed, have converged in the field of education. Her research focuses on proven technologies to enhance intelligence, abilities, and bliss.

With lots more to share, this promises to be the first of more books to provide inspiration and tools for your most desired Lifestyle.

www.ingramcontent.com/pod-product-compliance
Lightning Source LLC
Chambersburg PA
CBHW071742150426
43191CB00010B/1663